Raylynn's Dark Secret

By T. Kay Houston

www.raylynnsdarksecret.com

ISBN-13: 978-1483957500
ISBN-10: 1483957500

www.raylynnsdarksecret.com

Author T. Kay Houston
www.tkayhouston.com

Published by Michael Storzieri Jr.

Book Design by Mike Storzieri
www.smalltimemarketer.com

This book is dedicated to the wonderful understanding and compassionate man who pushed me in the direction of healing.

My counselor who helped me get the help I needed and to all of the survivors who have endured the trauma of abuse, domestic violence, and rape.

PREFACE

Every family has its secrets and most don't want to ever let these secrets out due to fear that it may destroy them. Often, I think about how telling a story about abuse and exposing the ugly truth to the world could really destroy anyone. I realized that the truth about the ugliness that exists within a family unit can destroy a persona, a family's protected story. It will expose the story of how the abusers work their dirty little schemes and can cause them great embarrassment when the truth about what they have done is exposed to the world. I am sure we all have something in our past that we have done that we are ashamed of. For the most part, I believe that those who are abusers, rapists, swindlers, and so on are more afraid of getting caught because they know what they have done has its consequences.

As I write this book, I consider the consequences of exposing the ugly truth that is out there and that it is not just my burden to bear. The one thing that keeps going through my mind is that this secret is not so secret because many victims have told the family secret to at least one person. Considering that more than one person has confronted the victim at one time or another, the family secrets are really not that secret at all because the truth shall always find a way out.

I have found that many gossips about various secrets. They often whisper and talk behind each others' back. It is one of those things that everyone already knows but are not supposed to talk about. These secrets are the ones that causes the room to hush when someone of subject walks in a room. I have found that even with in my own family; I am quite often the subject of interest with in my family. I used to feel sad and alone, much like an outcast that would never be accepted. Today as I embark on my own journey towards healing begins, I am going to begin writing this story. It is a story like many others with the one exception, I am willing to expose the act of violence of sexual assault to the world.

Many ask me why I want to tell this story and my answer is simple. I am a survivor of abuse and I am here to tell the world what it is like. This story is inspired by true stories of real victims and I plan to expose the act of abuse for what it is and encourage others to expose the truth about victims being assaulted. I have read some blogs and have read some books written by victims. I have even had some experiences of my own. It happens to more people, men and women alike, then reported. Every report should be handled as a true assault because for almost all are in fact true.

I am writing this book, not to destroy a family, not to give gossip to the world, but to expose one of the world's largest hidden problems in society today. It's a problem that gets overlooked because as long as no one speaks out loud or openly about it, nothing will have to be done about it. First I had to accept that the abuse I endured happened and that it was real and this is how recovery begins.

These issues need to be exposed and real true help needs to be available for the victims who turn to crime, drugs, alcohol and become the abusers of the future. True help needs to be available for the mentally ill and adult victims of child sexual assault. Acknowledging that the problem exists is the first step to reaching a solution. I am writing this book to give others like me an opportunity to heal, to give others who don't understand an opportunity to understand, and making the world aware that what we do to our children will impact their lives and in turn as a whole will affect society in general with the damaged, lost, souls the abuse creates.

Although this story is inspired by true events it is in fact only fiction none of the characters are real. They were created to tell the story about how these types of crimes affect the victims and to show that it is possible to find healing and to find happiness and be able to live fully in life once again although life will never be the same.

Chapter 1

Counseling and the Roofie

Raylynn twisted nervously in her seat as she waited to be called in for her first counseling appointment. Watching the clock on the wall as the hands ticked around to the next minute, she leans over to Reverend Joe to tell him this is a mistake, I shouldn't talk about the past. The Reverend looked at her sweetly with his puppy dog eyes, patted her hand and reassured her that she was doing the right thing. He told her this is how she will become whole again. Raylynn remembered the words of her minister so softly spoken last week that healing is the repair of a shattered soul. It is taking the time to pick up all of the shattered pieces and put them back together making the soul whole once again.

Suddenly the door to the back office swung open and a friendly young woman called her name. Raylynn being middle aged of 49 with a bit of age showing on her rugged face, she slowly stood up on her feet, brushed her long gray streaked hair out of her eyes and walked toward the young woman. As she moved closer, the woman smiled and introduced herself. Hi, I'm Sara, we spoke on the phone. I will be assessing your case to see if we can help you.

Raylynn shyly smiled back as she walked through the door. She followed Sara down the hall to a small office. Sara quickly unlocked the door and invited Raylynn in to have a seat.

Sara seemed very friendly and warm which made Raylynn feel a little more comfortable sitting there alone with her in this small room. The room was about 10 feet by 10 feet and unremarkable. Raylynn took a look around the room and seen that there was a computer on a desk to her left attached to a bookshelf with a few books on it that were psychology related. On the floor there was a small basket with a few toys in it.

Raylynn sat at a small round table across from Sara. There was a jar with some candy, a box of tissues, and some ink pens on the table. Raylynn was still a bit tense because she had no idea where to begin. Where should she start her story? She just sat quietly while Sara prepared to take notes and looked through Raylynn's file.

Sara began with a small introduction. She said, I am going to ask you some questions and I would like for you to answer them as honestly as you can. I am here to help you but I can only help you if you tell me what is really going on.

Tell me a little about yourself Raylynn. Why are you here? Raylynn sheepishly answered with, I have some problems that I don't know how to handle. She paused not knowing how to say it. She began to explain, I often have panic attacks, I have nightmares every night and have trouble sleeping. I have flashbacks that plague my waking hours while the nightmares destroy my nights. I was molested by my father when I was growing up and I have been raped more than once.

With the brief description and an acknowledgment that Raylynn suffers from Post Traumatic Stress Disorder, Sara politely asks Raylynn if she has any questions for her in return.

Raylynn thoughtfully considers any questions and decides to ask Sara about her background. Raylynn asks Sara confidently now that the session was coming to a conclusion. “What are your qualifications?” Sara smiled and answered with calm reassurance that she has a master’s degree in Psychology and although she graduated recently she is confident in her skills to be able to make a fair and accurate assessment. Sara explained that she likely would not be the counselor that Raylynn would be working with if her case is accepted in the program.

Raylynn, horrified at the thought of not being able to have Sara as her counselor quickly asked who would be her counselor. Sara’s reply was not very reassuring. Sara simply replied with, I don’t know at this point but we will let you know. It shouldn’t take too long. Sara began to explain “What is going to happen next is that I will take your case to the board and they will decide if we will take your case and then a decision will be made as to whom your counselor will be”.

Sara smiled and lead Raylynn back out to the waiting room where Reverend Joe was patiently waiting. Raylynn gives Sara a polite smile, says good-bye then turns to face Reverend Joe who was now approaching her. Raylynn thought to herself, there is no way I can do this. The Reverend noticed the expression of fear on her face and became concerned. He looked at her and asked if she was going to be alright. Raylynn nodded in agreement that she would be fine and they walked out of the office.

A week later, Raylynn was beginning to think that she was not going to get counseling. She was allowing the negative thoughts to tear at her as if they were truth. They will never approve me for counseling she thought to herself. Why would anyone want to help me? I am middle aged, poor white trash who has nothing to offer. I can't even make a donation.

She was standing off to the side while Reverend Joe purchases two cups of coffee. He was carrying one for him and one for her. They had this routine every Sunday and Wednesday afternoon to sit and have coffee while Reverend Joe talked to her about her troubles. Her cell phone began to ring. Startled by the surprise of the call she dropped the phone and by the time she picked it up, she had already missed it. A few minutes later she got the alert that she had a message. Not sure who had called, she listened to the message and it was Sara. Raylynn couldn't believe what she was hearing. Sara was calling to let her know that she has been approved for counseling.

It was going to start. It was really going to happen. She was actually going to see if there is a chance for her to heal and become a whole person. Maybe these jitters and flashbacks will go away. Reverend Joe walked up and seen the tears in Raylynn's eyes and became concerned. Who was it Raylynn? What's wrong? Raylynn looked up at him and told him that she was approved for counseling. Reverend Joe grinned from ear to ear and said "see, I told you, you will get the help you need".

Raylynn returned Sara's call as soon as possible and set up the appointment. Much to Raylynn's relief, Sara was going to be her counselor after all. Reverend Joe, being the sweet and charming minister of her church was in a cheery good mood as always. They walked over to a little table in the corner of the lobby. They were just getting comfortable when Raylynn looked him right in the eye and said, Reverend Joe, why do you want to help me so much? Why me?

As he sat down, he took a little sip of his hot coffee. He looked at her with a firm and sincere expression. Raylynn, I have a calling to help others. That is why I became a minister. I see something special in you, Raylynn. For some reason I have this feeling that I am supposed to help you and I know you are just as important as the others I have tried to help. Raylynn sat back in her chair and considered what the Reverend had said. I am special alright, she thought as she considered his words. She couldn't help but feel that there is more to it than he was letting on. She couldn't help the thought that he was after something, but what? What could he possibly want from her?

The rest of the visit was a bit drab as they discussed the sermon he was going to deliver that evening for the Wednesday night service. It was going to be another usual night at the church of the Rising Sun. There was going to be the monthly potluck after the service.

Raylynn, I want you to think deeply about your upcoming journey of healing that is about to begin. Try to think of ways that the Divine will be working in your life to help you overcome the darkness of your past that shadows over your present and keeps you from seeing a positive future. He went on and on, while Raylynn didn't want to seem rude, she was having a difficult time staying focused on the subject. She shook her head and said, what was that you were saying? He looked at Raylynn with sadness as he realized she was somewhere else, lost in her own world. Raylynn often drifted off into her own thoughts. She often wondered what life would have been like if she had been adopted into a loving and caring family.

He finally changed the subject and asked her if she was planning to bring anything for the potluck. She nodded and simply stated she was thinking about a 5 layer dip and chips. He smiled and said he was looking forward to trying her 5 layer dip. He heard some of the ladies in the church talking about how good of a cook she is. Raylynn looked at her watch and made an excuse to break away from the visit. She had to get ready for the service and finish the dip.

That evening Raylynn was deep in thought all night only half paying attention throughout the service. She sat quietly in a corner hoping that no one would talk to her because she simply was not in the mood for social jibber jabber. She stayed for a while and finally people were starting to leave and she quickly grabbed her dish with what was left, said her good nights and swiftly walked out of the social hall. She got in her car and sat the leftover dip and chips on the seat beside her. With both hands on the steering wheel she took a deep breath and exhaled with relief that the evening was finally over. Raylynn drove home wondering about Sara and the whole counseling idea.

The appointment with Sara was only a few days away. Raylynn was both anxious and excited about the upcoming appointment. What would Sara want to talk about? Will she expect to talk about the horrible details on the first visit? Will Sara believe her? Raylynn wasn't sure of what to expect. She was so afraid to talk about all the secrets since no one has ever taken her seriously or believed her before. She drove home lost in thought. She pulled into the parking lot of her apartment complex and sluggishly grabbed the dip, chips and her belongings and slowly walked up to her bottom floor apartment.

She dropped her keys as she was trying to unlock the door. Dang it! She exclaimed. Just at that moment, Barbara her next door neighbor walked up and picked up her keys. Hi Ray, you just getting in from church? She asked. Yep, Raylynn muttered. Here let me help you, Barbara said happily. Whatchya got in the dish Ray? She asked with curiosity as she unlocked the door then sat the keys down just inside the door on the key hook as she waited for an answer. 5 layer dip, or what's left of it anyway. What has you out this evening Barbara? Raylynn asked. Maria and I went to the movies tonight. Oh Raylynn replied. Well, aren't you the least bit curious about the movie we seen? Barbara asked. She was a bit confused because Raylynn usually wanted a whole description of the movies she would go to see. Raylynn just shrugged her shoulders and said, not tonight Barbara I am a bit tired.

I bet you are getting sick Ray. You should take it easy for a couple of days and take vitamins, Barbara said with a concerned look. Naw, I'm not getting sick, I just had a long day. Okay. Well, I'll let you settle in and rest then, and with that Barbara bounced out the door.

Raylynn closed the door and locked it as usual, put her things away and got ready for bed. She had a difficult time falling asleep that night with her mind racing with thoughts about what she was going to have to talk about at the next counseling session. She couldn't help but feel a little anxious about it. She closed her eyes and drifted off to sleep.

The night was filled with nightmares as usual and she didn't get much sleep. She woke up before the alarm went off just as the crazy man was about to stab her as the crowd of onlookers hissed "it is all your fault Raylynn, it's all your fault. The next few days went on as usual with nothing extraordinary happening. Raylynn tried not to think too much about the up and coming appointment with Sara.

On the day of her appointment with Sara, Raylynn was having second thoughts. Maybe I shouldn't go through with this. I don't think I can talk about these things. Sara is going to think I am lying like others have. Sara will know that I am a bad person and she is going to know how pathetic I am. She was startled by a gentle knock on the door. She sighed as she remembered Reverend Joe was going to pick her up. He volunteered to go with her for support. She knew it was his way of making sure she keeps her appointments with Sara.

As Raylynn walked to the door she tried to pull herself together even if only on the outside. As she reached for the doorknob she took a deep breath and smiled as she exhaled to put on that safe old happy face for Reverend Joe. She opened the door and there he stood with a pleasant smile on his face. Hello Reverend Joe, Raylynn said softly. Hi, Raylynn are you about ready? We need to get going in a few minutes. Don't want to be late on your first appointment he exclaimed happily as he stood in the doorway.

Umm, yes, I'm just about ready, I just have to grab a few things, Raylynn said with a smile. Come in for a minute Reverend while I grab my things. Do you want anything to drink? I have soda or tea or water if you like. Reverend Joe Looked at Raylynn, Her hair was pulled back with just a few wisps of hair falling around her face. She looked like she was okay but it just didn't seem like she was really okay. He had a vibe it was all just a cover for how she was really feeling.

How are you doing? I mean how are you really feeling at the moment, he asked. Oh I'm fine just a little nervous is all, she said with a hint of sweetness in her voice. We should probably be going, I'm ready, she said calmly. The whole trip to the clinic was in silence. Neither of them spoke a word. As Reverend Joe pulled into the parking lot to the New Rising hope clinic he looked over at Raylynn and could see that she was a little stressed out and lost in thought. We're here he said with a smile. Have you thought about what you want to talk to Sara about today? He asked while she took a deep breath and looked around. Her heart was beating a mile a minute as usual when she starts out with something new involving people she doesn't know. She half grinned and said yep, I have an idea of what I would like to talk about but we will see how it goes.

They both step out of the car and Raylynn stopped to pick up her purse and took a look at the building. It was just a small square building with double swinging doors. As she walked closer to the building she could see on the doors and it said, New Rising Hope clinic of Behavioral Health. Behavioral Health she thought. I guess my behavior is unhealthy with all of the anxiety and flashbacks. I must seem like a real freak to normal people.

Reverend Joe opened the door and motioned for her to step through. Raylynn took a look around as she walked in the front door. There was hardly anyone in the waiting area. She counted six people waiting. There are two people at the counter. She spotted the sign that read, wait here for next available aid. She walks over to stand behind the sign waiting to be motioned over to the counter. She noticed it smelled like paint and new carpet in the lobby as she waited.

Reverend Joe waited quietly behind her and Raylynn didn't pay much attention to him. One of the aids motioned for her to come forward. Raylynn felt stiff as she walked up to the counter. The woman behind the counter seemed friendly. She greeted

Raylynn with a smile. Hi, how can I help you today? The woman asked in a friendly yet mellow tone.

I'm Raylynn Buford and I'm here to see Sara, she said nervously. Raylynn fidgeted with her purse while the woman pulled up her name on the computer.

Okay Raylynn, go ahead and have a seat, I will let Sara know you are here, the woman said quietly with a smile. Reverend Joe took Raylynn by the arm as if to help her walk steady and escorted her to a seat near the back office door. Joe looked at Raylynn with a serious expression. He reached over and patted her hand. You will do fine Ray, don't worry. Sara will guide you and the words will come to you. Raylynn looked at him and sighed. She gave him a half smile and said I know, I'm just a little nervous.

A few minutes later, Sara opened the door and called her name. Raylynn looked at Reverend Joe with a sad look and he reached over and squeezed her hand. She got up and walked over to Sara. Sara smiled, said hello and asked how she was doing. I'm okay Raylynn said with a sheepish smile and her head down. They arrived at Sara's office and Sara quickly unlocked the door. They stepped inside and Sara invited Raylynn to have a seat.

They sat down at the little round table. Sara opened her notebook and prepared to get started. How are you feeling today Raylynn? She asked politely. I'm okay I guess Raylynn replied. Sara began as she sat comfortably across from Raylynn. So Raylynn, tell me a little about yourself.

Raylynn shifted in her seat as she thought carefully about what she was going to say. Raylynn began speaking softly. She felt as though her throat was going to squeeze closed and she wouldn't be able to speak.

I used to truly believe that my purpose on this planet was to satisfy the sadistic and twisted pleasures of everyone who crossed my path. Because the abuse started when I was just a toddler and it went on until I was about 30 something I truly believed that God hated me and wanted to punish me for some horrible thing I did in a past life. I believed that he cursed me to live a life full of hateful and horribly sick and twisted events. Sara listened quietly. Raylynn found herself sitting in a pool of self pity. For a while now, I have been struggling to get through a book a friend suggested I read accompanied by its partner the workbook. It was a book for survivors of child sexual abuse. My one question has always been why me? Why does this always happen to me? Do I have a sign on my forehead that says come rape me?

I went from the dirty clutches of my father to the sick and twisted grasp of abusive men in the world, I found myself struggling to survive another day and asking myself why I try to live on. My world has been a world of misery and by the time I hit 37 it had become a virtual prison that I desperately wanted to escape. The constant struggle with flashbacks, anxiety and sleepless nights brought me to a place where I found myself needing to be heavily sedated every night just to get a few hours of sleep.

I couldn't stand it any more and I had given up fighting against the abuse, against the world who wanted to punish me for some unknown crime that I must have committed in another life. I gave up trying to find happiness, peace or even my purpose of life. I was ready for death to take me, I prayed for deadly diseases and natural disasters to finish me off and let me finally have peace in death. When the conversations were about living forever I would always add I wouldn't want to live forever, I hope for a short life and I think death will take me soon. I hoped for death, wished for death and resigned myself to allowing myself to exist only until the day I could leave this disgusting world with all of the sick and twisted people in it. I felt that the world was a place I didn't belong. Good things never happen to people like me. There are those who live a life of blessed luxury and those who live an entire life of hardship, struggles and suffering. I was the latter of the two. I was here to suffer for my entire life and I couldn't understand how this happened to people.

Who makes the choice of who gets the good life and who gets the bad life? Is there a God who decides that? Does the cold and heartless Universe decide that some live beautiful lives while others live a life of tragedy? I have been told on many occasions our lives go according to our choices that we make. I somewhat believe that our choices guide our lives in a way but I didn't choose to be born into a family with an abusive mother and sexually perverse father. I didn't choose to be molested and I didn't choose to be left unprotected from all of the horror all my life. Sara sat there calmly as Raylynn spoke about her feelings and her life. Sara asked, Is this how you feel right now? Raylynn said yes, I still feel this way most of the time.

Sara asked if she had told anyone else about this before. Has she had any other counseling? Raylynn shook her head, indicating no that she hasn't. Solemnly she said, no I have talked to some friends about it though. Mostly they just shake their head and make excuses as to why they have to leave.

I suppose for some my story is horrifying and for some it is nothing, but for me it is life and I feel I have no choice in the matter. I was never protected and I never learned how to protect myself. For most of my life I didn't even believe I had a right to protect myself. I used to think, I am alone and no one understands what I am going through. I used to feel and sometimes still do feel that others will never understand how much it takes out of me to live every day of my life. To live with nightmares all night since I was a child to the anxiety attacks I experience throughout the day for no apparent reason. What I must look like to someone looking in from the outside.

Sara asked, when was the last time anyone hurt you? When was the last time one of these assaults took place? Raylynn was fighting back the tears as she continued to speak. The last time I was assaulted I was in my late thirties. Richard the man I was living with who was once my high school friend who already had children of his own by the time we moved in together, planned and executed the assault with a couple of his friends who helped him do it. He lured me to the scene of the crime and participated in drugging me so that they can video record the rape. I didn't discover that the rape was more than a twisted dream until a couple years later when an ex-boyfriend told me that he had seen the video of me on the internet. I was confused and didn't know what he was talking about until the day a good friend showed me the actual video.

I watched in disbelief as I was being raped on the screen in my drugged state of mind. I could not believe it was me in the video because I had no recollection of it. I watched it a few more times and came to terms that it was me, that it was real and that I was drugged. It was at that moment I realized what, when, where and how this took place. That last incident started so incidentally and unexpectedly. I trusted this man and had no idea he was this sick and twisted or even hateful. At first I couldn't understand why he did it but then I realized he hated women and I was the one he had chosen to punish because I was the one he controlled the least or at least that is why he said he was always treating me so badly.

Do you think you can tell me about it? What do you remember? Sara asked calmly in an interested tone. Raylynn continued on to tell the story of the last rape. Well, she said. I got together with my high school friend Richard after I left my husband Greg and when I moved in with Richard, he and his wife Theresa had been separated for a year or so. He said he didn't want to divorce her yet because she would take him for everything he was trying to hold on to. He didn't want to lose the house. He worked as a flagman for Road Construction and had quite a bit of money saved back from saving since he was in high school. I didn't put much thought into it because I had just left my husband and was not interested in getting married again anyway.

I was not divorced yet although I wanted to be. I had known this man for about 16 years, or at least I knew him 12 years before when we had met in high school in the group I hung out with. When I was 25 a friend had brought him over to my apartment when we considered going out the first time. I already had my own place and before we got too seriously involved he had moved on to another girl who was considerably younger than us. We had stopped hanging out at that time for a while then they got married a couple of years later. I married another friend in the group named Barry and we were married for about 4 years.

During that time he was physically and verbally abusive to me. Richard didn't rape me back then. In fact he didn't want anything to do with me when we were young. But my husband was handsome and I was in love and after about 4 years I had enough of the abuse and told him I wanted a divorce. He got angry and broke my arm when he twisted it behind my back. I didn't leave at that moment but I left about six weeks later after the cast was removed. I had another abusive relationship with yet another jerk of a guy that I thought I was in love with and hoped he loved me back.

That is another story for another time I think. Eventually I had met my second husband Greg and just 6 months later we married and 3 and a half years after that I escaped yet another abusive relationship. I left my second husband and got together with my high school friend whom I was convinced had changed for the better and finally I would be loved. It was great until we moved in together and he would often tell me that if we are still living together after the three year mark, I will be able to take half of everything just like his wife because of Palimony or something like that.

Then Sara asked, did you plan to take money from him after three years? Raylynn looked at her puzzled and replied, well no, I don't know why he thought about that. I didn't take anything from Barry when we got our divorce so he had no reason to think I would. At the time I didn't see that he didn't have any intentions of being with me long enough for me to qualify as a domestic partner. At the time I didn't put much thought into it because I figured we would not break up so it was irrelevant.

About the end of the first year of living with him, I began to realize that something was not quite right and sat down with him and told him I felt that it would be best if I moved out and we just stayed friends. I told him I am looking for a relationship with a guy who can care about me, wants to spend some time with me, respects my thoughts and opinions, and can sit and just chat with me. Bull shit sessions where we are not trying to work out problems, make financial plans or any other household business. I just want to talk about stuff that is fun, laugh and have a good time together.

At that time he said he wanted me to stay and got me to agree to play a family game with him and see if that would help me feel better about us and understand him more. I agreed and that was fine for a couple of months but then he decided he didn't want to play the game with me anymore. I was a bit disappointed but let it go. Then it just started to decline even further from there. He began to withdraw from me more and more over the second year. The third year was getting closer and he refused to let me purchase the food I liked to cook. He would not even let me go to the grocery store with him any more. I was no longer allowed to purchase health and hygiene products like shampoo, conditioner, deodorant or a toothbrush. He began doing things like calling me to tell me he was on his way home then not come home till the next day.

When I would call him a few hours later to find out what happened, he would start yelling at me and would call me a bitch. He would tell me to stop bitching at him and stop yelling at him and stuff like that. Sara asked Raylynn, were you yelling at him? Raylynn replied, no Sara, I didn't even raise my voice. Raylynn continued, this went on for a few months and I remember thinking, what the hell is wrong with this guy? One day he came home from work and said his friend Jack had invited us over for a dinner party. He worked with my boyfriend, he had a girlfriend, and they wanted to meet me.

I got dressed, did my hair, put on makeup and we went to their house. I walked in, met Jack and his girlfriend. We immediately had dinner on the back patio. That lasted about 20 minutes then we were rushed inside and a bottle of alcohol was brought out. His friend offered me a drink and because I don't drink

I politely declined. The friend began to pour on the peer pressure for me to have a drink.

Richard my boyfriend and his friend Jack were trying to tell me it tasted delicious like chocolate cake and I know better than to believe that booze taste good because I don't like the taste of alcohol. I can always taste the alcohol and find it repulsive. My boyfriend got upset and said, see I told you man, she won't drink. His friend quickly said, relax Man, it's okay, she will have a drink. Just one drink. I looked at Richard and back at his friend Jack and at his girlfriend. At this point Sara asked if she remembered Jack's girlfriend's name. Raylynn said she didn't. Go on Raylynn, Sara said. I thought for a minute and decided that I have known Richard for over 16 years; he would never do anything to hurt me. He is not a bad guy just because he doesn't get along with me.

I looked at Jack and thought, he seems like a nice guy and he has a girlfriend. His girlfriend seemed nice. I thought well, what harm could one drink do? Not like one drink is gonna get me drunk or cause me to be vulnerably intoxicated. I finally gave in and said okay. I'll try it, I'll have one shot. I took the shot, it was just as nasty as I thought it would be and tasted nothing like anything yummy. I said I did not want any more, I was done. It was so yucky and bitter tasting. He began harassing his girlfriend to take a drink of it. Jack told her not to let me drink alone. She protested, I heard her say that every time she drinks that stuff she passes out and doesn't feel good the next day.

In just a few minutes I began to feel a bit woozy. Light headed. I began to feel like I was going to pass out. I walked over to the sofa and sat down. I was feeling quite unusually intoxicated as I seen Jack's girlfriend was feeling the same way as she stumbled over to the chair across from me. A Roofie Sara thought. Raylynn said, he slipped me a Roofie.

8 hours later, I came to. Richard and Jack were playing a game on the play station, the girlfriend was still passed out in the chair and we were both covered with a blanket. I was confused; my thoughts a little muddled and were confused with why I had such crazy dreams. They both looked at me with a weird grin on their face. I asked for the time, it was 1:30 am. The last time I looked at my watch it was 5:30pm and that was right before I took that shot. I pulled myself together the best that I could and we left. On the way out the door I apologized to Jack for passing out. He chuckled and said don't worry about it because my girlfriend passed out too.

On the way home Richard asked me if I had a good time. I responded with, umm, I was passed out all night, I feel like I have been slipped a Mickey. If that is what you consider a good time then yeah. I was still groggy and my mind was still a bit hazy. I was still a bit confused.

I heard him on the phone the next day tell someone on the other end that I seem to have no recollection of what happened. I asked him, "So, what did happen last night?" He replied, what do you remember? I don't remember anything, I replied. His response was, "then nothing happened". A couple of weeks later, he did what he had done before. He called me at 6pm and said he was on his way home. He will be home shortly.

Three hours pass and I call his cell. When he answered I asked him what happened, why he isn't home yet. He said he was at a party and he would be home when he felt like it. I told Richard I did not like the way he was treating me. I told him I felt that it is unfair and that I had a problem with it. I did not yell or raise my voice. I said it matter of fact. He yelled at me as usual to stop being such a bitch and to stop bitching at him and that he can do whatever the hell he wants to do. I said, fine same to you, I am going to bed. I hung up. I went to bed and he came in around 2 am and very intoxicated. He would always drive while he was so intoxicated that he swerved and stuff.

I woke up at 6am the next morning, got up, logged on to the computer and started browsing some websites. He got mad that I woke him up and told me to get out of the house right now. He wanted me gone in an hour. I finally found some resources and managed to find a way out of that disgusting mental ward house and got away from that narcissistic, controlling, crazy, abusive jerk.

A couple years later, a friend of mine showed me a video. It was an amateur sex video on an amateur porn site. It was me and some guy I never met, I was wearing a shirt I have never seen before, in a room I have never been. Once I realized it was me, I also seen a bruise on my inner thigh that gave me the time-line of the incident. I thought back and realized that the only time in my entire life that I had lost time was that night at Jack's house. I also realized that the dreams I had, were not dreams at all and the video proved it. I later realized that I remembered how my dear boyfriend was struggling to get me to walk and Jack took over and I remember seeing the three men in the room and I was confused as to what I had seen. Richard and Jack were standing behind the camera watching the whole thing. Tears streamed down Raylynn's cheeks.

Sara stopped Raylynn at that point. I'm Sorry Raylynn, we are just about out of time and we need to schedule the next appointment. Do you mind if we stop there and pick up at the next visit. Raylynn said umm, no I guess I don't mind. Talking about this stuff is a bit difficult for me. I know, Sara replied, we will talk about it next week. Raylynn took a few deep breaths and pulled herself together.

When would you like to come back? I have Monday at 2pm, Wednesday at 10am, and Friday at 4pm. Raylynn thought for a moment and remembered that Reverend Joe was going to escort her to all of her counseling appointments, at least for a while. Raylynn chose Friday at 4pm so that she could get through her day before having to face these demons.

They planned out the next visit then Sara walked Raylynn out to the waiting room where Reverend Joe was waiting patiently as he had done before. Sara and Raylynn said their good-bye and Raylynn walked over to Joe who was now standing and wiping the sleep out of his eyes since he had dozed off for a minute. He looked at Raylynn's face and asked her, you okay Ray?

She said yep, I'm just fine. Good, good, said the Reverend as he walked her to his 82 ford escort that was donated to the church by a church member last year. He opened her door and helped her in the car. He hurried to the driver's side of the car and quickly got in.

He buckled his seat belt and looked over at her. Raylynn with her head down and her hair now down and covering her face he couldn't tell if she was going to be okay or not. He thought a minute and said, I'm starving I could use a bite to eat; you wanna go get some dinner Ray? She looked over at him and he was looking at her with those puppy dog eyes and his usual smile. Sure, she replied. I am a little hungry I guess. Raylynn tried to smile back at him but she just wasn't feeling it.

Alright then, How about Jim's burgers? Raylynn nodded and said that's fine. The rest of the way they sat quietly until they arrived at Jim's. As the Reverend turned off the engine and unbuckled his seat belt he could tell that Raylynn wasn't feeling very happy. Do you want to talk about it? He asked softly, as he reached over and squeezed her hand. Raylynn felt overwhelmed by all of the emotions that were stirred up and the images of the last rape kept running through her mind. I don't know if you can handle it Reverend she said sadly.

You would be surprised what sort of details I have heard in my life Ray, I'm sure I can handle it. Give me a try, he replied. Okay, do you remember me telling you that I was drugged and raped? Raylynn asked. Yes, I do Ray, he replied softly. I was telling her about that and I can't stop it from going through my head over and over now, she said with a frustrated tone. What do you remember about it? I am surprised you remember anything considering you were drugged. He said calmly. Well, I remember stuff before and after pretty clearly and I keep having these brief flashbacks that must have been during, you know, she said sadly. I am all ears if you want to talk about what you remember, Reverend Joe said with a sincere expression. Okay, she said, but don't be surprised if it gets to be too much for you. It won't be too much for me Raylynn; I've heard some pretty bad stuff. Go ahead, don't worry, I promise I won't be shocked about any of the details.

Okay, well, I remember right before I "passed out" Jack was telling Richard he had done it before. I remember my boyfriend Richard, trying to get me to walk down a hall and getting frustrated because I would not cooperate and walk for him. I remember his friend, Jack, putting his arm around me with his hand under my left armpit to hold me up. I remember his friend patting my left leg and telling me to move this leg forward, and then he did the same with the right. I remember lying down in a bed and looking off to my right and seeing Richard and Jack standing there grinning with their arms folded and giving each other a strange look.

I remember seeing this other guy that I didn't recognize but I couldn't figure out what he was doing. I recall feeling him doing things to my body and I could not push him away, although I wanted him to stop. I didn't know who the third guy was until after I had seen the video 3 years later. I remember enough to know what happened and I know I should have reported it. I remember enough to report it. I was told that I should report it because if every girl reports the same guy, it will make it easier to build a case against the guy or in my case, guys. The sad thing is I was Roofied so that my boyfriend could make a revenge video to put on the internet, most likely to humiliate me or to perpetuate the abuse he had already been doing. It was not about sex at all. Sex was just a tool they used to hurt me. The thing that bothers me the most is this wasn't the first time that a man has hurt me like that. It has been happening all of my life. I just don't understand why they pick me to do this to.

Did Sara say anything about why this keeps happening to you Ray? The Reverend asked. Not yet she replied. We haven't really gotten into anything like that yet. I just started telling her about myself.

Well, let's go get something to eat and talk about something else to get your mind off of things. Okay, she said as they both got out of the car. As they walked toward the diner door Raylynn said, I don't see how talking about all of this stuff is supposed to help. I mean it just seems to make me feel worse afterward. I know it seems that way right now Ray, but it will get better; you will see said Reverend Joe. You will see, just stick with it. He reached up and squeezed her shoulder as they walked through the door.

They both ordered Jim's Giant Bacon cheeseburger with a coke. They talked about the Sunday sermon and how life has its little quirks. They laughed a little at

Reverend Joe's jokes and Raylynn's mind was off of the past at least for a little while.

Chapter 2

Crazy Killers and Scary Dreams

The following week was even more difficult than usual. She couldn't help but feel a bit melancholy as she went about her routine. Work was long and tedious while the nights were filled with horrible nightmares that left her feeling tired and wrung out in the morning. I feel worse than usual she thought as she was getting ready for work. It's been 4 days since the last session and I am not feeling better talking about this stuff.

The nightmares are worse and I feel worse during the day. I don't know if I can go through with this any more. It just makes me feel so horrible and I feel so depressed all the time, she thought to herself. She couldn't shake the negative feelings as she thought about the counseling sessions to come and how they will compare with the one she already had. She couldn't shake the thoughts about the last rape and the dreams of her confronting Richard about it and how the dream always turned dismal with him trying to kill her and others helping him. Chasing her down like an angry mob.

The crazy men in her dreams seemed to always want to kill her. They always chased her with sharp daggers or some other sharp object. Once she had a dream that a crazy man was chasing her and trying to kill her by stabbing her eyes out with an ink pen.

Everyone she stopped and asked for help turned against her and said the man was a good man and how dare she say horrible things about such a good man. He wouldn't hurt a fly, they would say to her. The outsiders whom she stopped to ask for help in her nightmares didn't always chase her or try to help the crazy man but they wouldn't help her either. No one was going to save her. She always barely escaped the stabs of the crazy man in the dream. She always stayed just out of his reach barely surviving as the tormenting dreams continued.

She went to work as usual and the day crept by ever so slowly as she watched the clock. What seemed like hours were only a few minutes. It was slow in the store today. There was hardly a customer an hour. Could the day get any worse she thought? It seemed like the day would never end. Finally it was 4pm and time for her to go home. It was Wednesday and she knew it was time to meet with Reverend Joe. How he roped her into meeting with him twice a week and letting him drive her to all of her counseling appointments she never knew it was coming.

Before she knew it, it was set. She had to admit he has been quite helpful and she is beginning to look forward to their meetings. He has become a good friend. He is probably just lonely since he lives alone and doesn't seem to have many friends outside the church. She hurried out of the door and rushed home as quickly as she could. She met with Reverend Joe at 5:30 pm every Wednesday at the Dark Roast Coffee House. They had great coffee and served decent cold sandwiches for a reasonable price. It's perfect for a quick bite before Wednesday night service. Wednesday nights were informal church meetings. Mostly like a little social gathering. Reverend Joe would take donations and make announcements after his short speech on whatever topic he felt compelled to give that night.

She pulled in the parking lot of her apartment complex and parked a little crooked. She wasn't concerned about what the neighbors would say because she would be leaving again soon anyway. She rushed inside and quickly showered, pulled her hair back and put on her old dress. She stopped as she passed her full length mirror and thought; I really need to get a new dress. This old thing is getting so worn out. She was running out of time, she had to finish quickly and get out the door, it is almost 10 after 5 and if she didn't get to the coffee house soon, she was going to be late.

She pulled in front of the Coffee House right at 5:30. There was Reverend Joe sitting right out front waiting for her. She quickly got out of the car and grabbed her purse. She locked the door to her little white 1985 Pontiac Fiero. It was clean but had seen better days. She walked up to Reverend Joe and said, Hi, I hope you haven't been waiting long as she reached out to shake his hand. Naw, he said almost flirtatiously. I just got here about 3 minutes ago. Raylynn smiled shyly. She wasn't sure why but for some reason she felt a little embarrassed with his response. Joe quickly said, come on Ray; let's go get that cup of coffee and a sandwich before we have to go to church. They only had an hour on Wednesday night because Reverend Joe had to be at the church by 7pm to unlock the doors and get everything ready for the 7:30 meeting.

He told Raylynn to pick a table, so she walked over and sat down at the table next to the window. She loved being able to see out the window and watching everyone going about their day. She sat there patiently watching all the cars drive by getting home from work or running their evening errands. She wondered where everyone was going. She watched a young woman with her little girl get into a car. They were carrying shopping bags from the fashion store next door. A man walked in the door and walked up to stand in line behind Reverend Joe who was now getting ready to bring the coffee.

Raylynn watched him as he picked the packets of sugar and creamer and put them in his shirt pocket. He was of average height with a strong build. He was a little pudgy around the middle but overall quite handsome. She wondered why he wasn't married as he walked toward her with his hands full of hot steaming cups of coffee. He caught eyes with her and smiled. She looked down as if she were caught checking him out and grinned then looked back up at him.

He sat the coffees down on the table and emptied his pocket which was full of the sugar and creamer. As he sat down, he asked how she had been this week. Not bad she replied. I have to admit I don't think counseling is going to work for me. I feel worse than I did before and I am dreading the next appointment on Friday. It will seem to get worse at first, he said. Don't worry Raylynn it will work out. It will get better after awhile, you will see. I hope so Reverend because I really need some sleep, she said in a whisper. Ah, the nightmares still bothering you at night? He asked. Yes, and they seem to be worse this week and the anxiety is worse too, She said. Well, maybe you just need to eat better he told her as the woman behind the counter called his name. Reverend Joe pointed at the counter and said, I'm gonna go grab those sandwiches, I'll be right back. Raylynn nodded.

He quickly came back with a tray with two ham and cheese sandwiches on it. He always walked with a bounce in his step. She noticed he always seemed so happy. He was always smiling. What could make someone so happy she wondered as she watched him carry the tray? Reverend, what keeps you so happy? She asked as he sat the tray on the table. Ray, just call me Joe, he said. We are friends, no need to be so formal. Well? She persisted. Well what? He asked. Why are you always so happy? She insisted he answer her question. Well, I have a good church, I get to do what I love, and I have a great friend. He replied.

Why aren't you married? Surely someone had to be interested in you at some point, right? She asked with curiosity. I was married once he said. We were married for 26 years and one day she just up and left. She didn't say good-bye, or anything. I came home and she was gone, He said with a tone of sadness in his voice. You don't know why she left? Did you have a fight or anything? Raylynn asked. No, Ray, she just left. I suppose I will never know why. He said quietly. I'm sorry Rev... I mean Joe, she said.

Why do you want to know Ray? He asked. I was just curious as to why you were um... alone is all. She stammered. Okay Ray, fair enough, he said. Now eat your sandwich. I have to go soon. It's almost 6:35. He said solemnly. They both finished their sandwich and left feeling a bit melancholy that night. Raylynn had to stop for gas and picked up a card from the little convenient store where she worked. She hoped it would cheer Reverend Joe up after she ruined his mood this afternoon. She arrived at the church about quarter past 7 and there were already a few church members hanging around. She walked up to Reverend Joe and handed him the card with a smile. Cheer up Joe, she said. You still have me to look after, ya know.

Reverend Joe smiled at Raylynn making her feel a bit flushed. I know Ray, I'm fine really, it has been awhile since she left, he said as he placed a couple of candles on the table next to the incense. Gerty and Rosa a couple of the older women were standing nearby watching Ray and Reverend Joe. They were whispering about the two like school girls gossiping about classmates. Gerty whispered, rumor has it that they have been spending a lot of time together lately. Rosa asked quietly, do you think they are dating? I don't know but I think they would make a cute couple. Reverend Joe needs someone to look after him. Gerty replied.

Tom, one of Reverend Joe's friends walked up. Hi Joe, Hi Raylynn. Hi Tom, Raylynn said as she made an excuse to go sit down and wait for the service to begin. Tonight's meeting seemed rather long and boring.

Raylynn couldn't help but drift off into thought about what has happened in her life. She wondered why all those things have happened to her. Am I a bad person, she thought to herself. After the meeting she quickly sneaked out and went home. Thursday zoomed by like lightning and before she knew it, Friday was here.

Friday morning she got up after a night full of bad dreams and got ready for work. She had her appointment with Sara in the afternoon and would be getting off of work early today. She only works 5 hours on Fridays which made it easier to make her counseling appointments. She didn't want everyone at work knowing she was seeing a counselor. In fact she felt the fewer who knew she was in counseling the better she felt about it. It's bad enough people already treated her like she was a nut bar when she would have the anxiety attacks.

She arrived at work 3 minutes before 8am and the store manager Steve sniped at her about almost being late. Raylynn was usually 10 minutes early but today she had a difficult time getting motivated. The bad dreams seemed to be worse and she felt worse too. Dreading the counseling appointment and not knowing what she was going to talk about she didn't know what to expect. It just seemed that talking about the horrible past was just going to make things worse for her. The day went by quickly and Raylynn left work feeling a bit better than when she arrived. She went home and lay down for a while to simply relax before getting ready for the appointment with Sara.

She laid there on her bed trying to think happy thoughts about things she would like to do. Forming a little bucket list of things she hasn't done that she would really like to do someday. She thought about what it would be like to travel the world and take pictures of all the beautiful places around the world. She wondered what kind of wild animals and bugs were in a tropical rain forest and found herself thinking of one of the most beautiful places she had been. It was a place in Colorado. Although she couldn't remember the name of the place she remembered the hills and the trees. The air was crisp and she could remember the smells of the pine trees and all the echoing noises that she had heard up there on the trails. It was spring and there were still little patches of snow on the ground.

She loved to go hiking when she was young and usually found some of the best trails. She glanced over at the clock and it was already 3. Oh crap she thought. I had better get ready to go and do it quickly. I hope Reverend Joe is late today, she thought as she quickly took off her work uniform. She felt behind on everything all day. She let her hair down and quickly brushed it then she brushed her teeth and washed her face. She wanted to put makeup on but didn't have much time so she wasn't going to be wearing any today. She threw her jeans and a t-shirt on and figured that would be just fine for a day like today.

She was on her way to the kitchen when she heard Reverend Joe knock on the door. She walked to the door, took a deep breath, put on her smile and then opened the door. Hi Joe, come on in, I'm almost ready, she said. Reverend Joe walked in the door and stood by the sofa. He cleared his throat and asked Raylynn how she was doing. Oh fine I guess, just a little behind today she replied. Reverend Joe watched Raylynn race around the apartment gathering her hair tie, purse and her shoes. So, why are you so behind? He asked patiently. I don't know, just a little tired I guess. I didn't sleep well last night, she replied as she hastily put on her shoes. Okay I'm ready let's get out of here, she exclaimed. Relax Ray, we will get there on time, don't worry, he said as he slowly walked out the door.

He walked her to his car and helped her in. He smiled at her as he closed the door causing her to blush. She always felt so warm when he smiled at her. He walked around and got in the car and buckled his seat-belt. Buckle up Ray, it's the law, he joked with a hint of seriousness. She buckled her seat-belt and they were on their way to her appointment. They sat in silence almost halfway there when she blurted out, you don't have to drive me all the time you know. I can drive myself to my own appointments. He replied, I know, I just want to make sure you get there and can get home okay. I know how stressful these sessions can be sometimes. Besides Ray, I think it does you some good to spend some time with a real person and I don't mind the company either.

She nodded half listening while looking out the window. She was thinking about what Sara was going to talk about today. What should I say to her? Raylynn wondered as she watched the world go by as she stared out the window.

Reverend Joe pulled into the parking lot of the clinic. We're here, he said as he parked right in front of the building. Raylynn looked up at the little square building. She wondered as she got out of the car if she would ever feel better about these counseling sessions. She started to feel a little anxious as they walked toward the front door. What would it be like today she wondered? Should she lay it all on her today? Should she talk about the other times she was raped or should she talk about the abuse as a child? She wasn't sure how this session was going to turn out.

They stepped inside and there was a short line waiting to check in. Raylynn walked over to the end of the line and Reverend Joe followed behind her. Joe, you can go find a seat for us if you'd like. You don't have to wait in line with me, I will be fine, Raylynn said softly. Okay Ray, he replied, I'll go sit down. Raylynn watched Reverend Joe as he walked over to a seat in the corner. He walked with his usual bounce. He is such a nice guy she thought to herself. He looked up and caught her looking at him. Embarrassed, she quickly looked away. Reverend Joe grinned and sat quietly as he waited for Raylynn to check in.

The line moved quickly and Raylynn checked in with in a few minutes. She walked over to Reverend Joe and sat next to him. How you feeling Ray, he asked with concern. I'm fine she replied with a half smile. It does get better, you will see. You just have to get to know Sara a little better then you will feel more comfortable with her. Raylynn smiled weakly and nodded.

Sara promptly called her name and as Raylynn stood up her body felt like lead. She felt stiff and her palms were a little wet with sweat. As she approached Sara, Raylynn smiled the best she could but her face felt frozen and she imagined she looked a little goofy trying to smile. Sara smiled back and said, Hi Raylynn how are you doing today? Good she replied quickly. They talked about the hot weather and how nice the fall will be when it finally gets here as they walked to Sara's office. Once inside her little office Sara asked Raylynn how she has been doing for the past week. Raylynn began by telling her that the dreams have gotten worse and she hasn't had much sleep. The sleeping pills help but she is still having trouble with the dreams waking her up several times throughout the night. She explained how she has been feeling down this week and that the rapes have been on her mind more often these last few days. Sara listened silently as Raylynn spoke about the last week and how difficult it had been.

When Raylynn was finished Sara said that it would help if Raylynn made a time line of her life from when she was born until now to see what has happened in her life so that they can get a better look at how her life has progressed. Raylynn wasn't sure what she was supposed to put on it or how it was supposed to look and her confusion must have shown on her face because Sara began to describe what sort of stuff to put on the time line and gave her some suggestions of how she could create it. Sara explained why it would be a good idea to do the time line and that it is important to do the homework she assigns her because it is to help her with healing.

It is important to try to do the work because healing has to come from within herself. She essentially has to do the work to help the healing take place. Raylynn was a little worried about how thinking about all of these things were going to make her feel over the next week. Here she is in her mid 40's and a lot has happened over her lifetime. She wasn't sure she was going to remember everything. Sara gave her some sheets with instructions for the time line then they scheduled the next 4 appointments. All of the appointments were going to be at the same time on the same day of the week. So every Friday at 4pm for the next four weeks were going to be spent here at the New Hope Clinic.

They walked out to the waiting room where Reverend Joe was waiting patiently. Raylynn folded the papers in her hand as she walked toward him. Are you ready to go Raylynn? He asked as she approached him. She said yes let's get going and they left the clinic. On their way to her house he asked her how it went and she said it went fine. Not as bad as she thought it was going to be. Reverend Joe just smiled and kept driving.

They arrived at her apartment and Reverend Joe walked her to her door. Thanks Joe for being there for me. No problem Ray, I don't mind at all, He replied. So what are those papers all about? He asked. It's my homework, she said. Oh, what is it? He pried a little more to find out what she had to do for her homework. I have to make a time line of my life, she said. Well, take your time with it Ray; do a little at a time over the next few days. Don't wait 'til the last minute to get it all done, He warned. I won't wait until the last minute, she replied. Okay, I have to get going Ray, He said. I have to meet with Tom in an hour. We are going to go over some stuff for a project he is working on for his son this Yule. He only has five months left to work on it before Yule and it is going to take a while to finish this project, he said. What is he making? She asked. I promised him I wouldn't tell anyone what it is going to be but I know his son is going to love it, any teenaged musician would. He replied.

Okay, I've said enough already. I'll see you later Ray. Take care and I'll see you on Sunday. He said with a smile. Okay Joe, See you Sunday, she said as he walked away. Raylynn went in and turned on her computer so that she can get a file started for her new time line homework.

Chapter 3

The Church

Raylynn sat at her old computer trying to remember events from the time she was born. How early do my memories go back? Let me think, what is the earliest memory I have? Hmmm, okay, so I would start with my birth since that was significant. Oh yes I remember my second birthday. Someone was asking me how old I was. I remember holding up two fingers or at least trying to. Raylynn remembered things that she didn't even know she remembered. She started making her time line. She got to some difficult memories of the abuse as a small child. Man I don't even know how old I was when it all started. It must have begun before my second birthday she thought.

Some of the early memories didn't seem bad but they were always followed by a bad memory. She worked on her time line for a while but then she began to feel very tired. It was emotionally draining to think about all of those difficult memories. As she began to go down memory lane it felt as though she was reliving the experiences all over again. As if she was there and it was happening again right then and there.

She began to cry. How could anyone do that to a child she thought as she remembered the man in the house next door licking his daughters face as she cried for him to stop. Man that little girl must have been 2 years old. It seemed to be happening all around her while she was growing up. It wasn't just happening to her, other men were doing it to their daughters too. How can they do that? She thought again. She was sure she would never understand how any grown adult can see a child as a sexual object.

It was beginning to make her feel sick so she saved her file and closed it. She couldn't do any more of the time line at that moment. I'm never going to get this homework done she thought to herself. I just can't do this. It is too much, too hard to do. She got up and walked into the bedroom and changed her clothes put on her pajamas and got ready for bed. She walked into the bathroom and started to brush her teeth. She looked in the mirror and found herself reliving another flashback.

She was brushing her teeth but she was a little girl. She was standing on a little stool and could barely see in the mirror. She remembered she couldn't see her chin and barely could see her upper row of baby teeth when she stood on her toes. Then she saw her father walk in and close the door behind him. He walked over to her and reached up her little nightgown then as suddenly as it started the flashback ended. Raylynn began to cry because she remembered what happened after he closed the door. She remembered as always the look of intent on his face. She sat on the floor and sobbed for a while with her face in her hands and toothbrush in her lap. She hated what he did to her.

The next morning she woke up from yet another horrifying nightmare. She woke up feeling terrified and very much alone as she usually does in the morning. She looked at the clock to see what time it was. The alarm was going to go off in 10 minutes so she reached over and turned off the alarm and crawled out of bed.

The day went by just as horrible as the night. She had to work another half day today. She hated working on Saturdays but she needed Friday to be a half day and she needed the hours. She didn't try to work on the time line after work and figured she would work on it a little on Monday or next week sometime. She just couldn't face any more new memories today. The flashbacks haunt her as if she is being ripped through time to relive the dreaded moments over again. Sunday morning she woke up from the usual nightmares and sat in bed for a minute. She had to meet with Reverend Joe that afternoon. She always had off on Sundays.

She made herself some whole wheat toast and washed some strawberries and blueberries to eat for breakfast. She always loved to eat fruit mixed with whipped cream in the morning. She showered and got dressed then she brushed her teeth and finished getting ready to go meet with the Reverend. She still had 3 hours before she was expected to meet with him for lunch. On Sunday morning Reverend Joe was working at the Homeless shelter trying to help those who found themselves in a dire situation. He would help them get set up with some resources that were available and help those in need of counseling get set up at the New Hope Clinic since they offered an array of mental health services for the homeless and the working poor.

One o'clock was getting closer and it was about time to get over to the Dark Roast coffee house. Raylynn gathered her things and locked the door on her way out. She arrived at the coffee house just a few minutes early and Joe was late for a change. He was usually early and waiting on her to arrive. I wonder what is keeping him. She thought as she looked through her purse for some lip gloss. Reverend Joe was almost 15 minutes late. She started to see dancing stars and the moon was singing, suddenly she was startled by a knock on her window. She realized she must have dozed off for a minute or two. She got out of the car and Reverend Joe was already apologizing for being late. I'm sorry I'm late Ray. I got caught up at the shelter, he said meekly. Don't worry about it Joe, she replied. I know how your work can take time. Did everything work out OK? She asked knowing he couldn't discuss the details. I think so, he replied skeptically.

I'm starving Ray; I didn't have time to eat breakfast. Let's get inside and get our order in. They walked inside and there was a bit of a line. They walked to the back of the line and waited together. So how have things been for you so far this weekend? He asked. I have been having some trouble sleeping these last couple of nights. I'm a bit tired but I guess I am fine. She replied.

She was lost in thought before she knew it. Ray! Reverend Joe exclaimed as he tapped her shoulder. Huh? What? She replied. I asked how you were doing on your time line. He said with a degree of frustration.

What's on your mind? He asked. Oh the usual stuff. Just a bit tired and off focus, she replied matter-of-factly. Well, how is your time line coming along? He asked again. Fine, I got some of it done. Still have about 30 years to cover. I see, he said, you know if you don't do your homework you will not be able to stay in the program, he said with concern. I know Joe, I will get it done, don't worry. It is just a bit difficult to remember that far back. She said flatly.

Do you want the usual Ray? He asked. Sure, she said, with no mayo please. Okay Ray, why don't you go find us a seat and I will take care of the order, He said as he motioned to a corner with a couple of empty tables. Raylynn nodded and picked the table closest to the window. She was soon lost in thought once again. How am I ever going to get through this if I can't even do a simple time line? She thought. It seems to make everything worse. The flashbacks, the anxiety and even the nightmares are worse. She was brought back to the present when Reverend Joe sat the cup of coffee in front of her and began to empty his pocket of the cream and sugar.

What has got you so wrapped up in thought today Ray? He asked as he sat down. She looked up at him and tried to smile. This whole time line business has me remembering a lot of things Joe. Things I have forgotten. She replied. Good things? He asked. Not all of the memories are good but some are not so bad, she replied with a sigh. Well, you should put it all down on paper so that you can be done with it. He said matter-of-factly. I know, I will. She gave Joe a half smile. She picked at her sandwich but wasn't feeling very hungry while Joe ate his sandwich without stopping to say a word. They sat in silence while eating their lunch. Raylynn seemed to be feeling worse every day. The depression was really starting to weigh her down like she was carrying a pocket full of rocks.

They sat and visited for about an hour discussing the sermon Reverend Joe was going to give that night. They talked about the hot summer weather and what their favorite foods are. After the meeting with Joe, Raylynn went home and just laid down on her bed thinking about the time line. She wondered just how much stuff to put on her time line and just how much to say about it. She hated having to think so much about the past. Her past has not been the brightest and happiest times of her life. In fact, there were few bright or happy times in her life. She laid there and tried to block out the bad memories with thoughts of where she would like to go someday. England would be a great place to go visit she thought. I wonder if Stonehenge is an awesome place to visit she thought out loud as she tried to focus on stuff that made her smile. She had a difficult time blocking out the bad stuff. A bad memory always crept its way into her thoughts taking away her smile.

It was time to get ready for the Sunday service so she got up and put on her old dress. It was the only dress she owned. She always wore it to church on Sundays and Wednesdays. She liked wearing a dress because it made her feel feminine to wear a dress and she felt safe at church. The Church of the Rising Sun was not the average church. It was not even a Christian church. It was more of a place to go and socialize and get help when one needed it. This church was more for those who loved the earth and Mother Nature and Just wanted to live life as close to what was natural as one possibly could. Reverend Joe wasn't the average Christian Reverend who preached about hell and sin but he talked more about life, love and making peace with one's self.

Of course like most churches, drugs and irresponsible behavior and anything that was harmful to the human body was frowned upon. Teaching that harming themselves or others was a path to self destruction and unhappiness. One should focus more on healing themselves and being helpful to those around them. It was not so much a religion as it was a way of living and thinking. Of course the church had its rituals and ceremonies such as weddings and giving thanks to the Gods but it was very different from the Christian church Raylynn grew up with.

Women were treated as equals and there were female clergy members in the church that also lead services. Often there were activities during the warmer months that took the members outside in the open doors of nature. The church had an outdoor sanctuary that was full of lovely plants and shrubs. There were vines on the walls that enclosed the sanctuary. There was a stone pulpit in the center where the Reverend who was leading the gathering would stand and lead the meeting. Raylynn loved that about this church. They never tried to recruit new members but always accepted new members with open arms. They knew that their way of life was not for everyone and that was okay with them. They were perceived as strange and that was alright with all of the old members who were comfortable with the loving kindness that was given freely to others. Of course, they were also very protective of their members as well. If anyone was to try to harm a member the whole church would stand up and protect the member. The church members would never stand in the way of the law when it came down to broken laws because the church teaches that there are consequences for one's actions.

Reverend Joe spoke well that night and Raylynn was relieved that she was not bothered so much by the memories while at church. A few of the other ladies were there to chat with and they kept her mind off of things for a little while after the service. Sandra a young woman in the church that has been friends with Raylynn for the last year was there that night. She ran up to Raylynn and Shrieked Ray! My best friend! Ray turned to see her running up to her with her arms stretched out. She ran up and hugged Ray. Raylynn stood there and not knowing what else to do she hugged her back. Hi Sandra, Ray exclaimed. Where have you been? Ray asked politely. I have been at my Aunts house for the last two months. I have been helping out. She had to have surgery and couldn't take care of herself very well. Sandra replied. So what has been up with you Ray, you look like you haven't slept in days, She said with concern as she put her hand on Rays forearm. Oh you know, I have been really busy and haven't had much time to sleep with work and all. Raylynn replied as she patted Sandra's hand.

Well, I had better get going Ray said as she fumbled with her keys. Yeah, it was good to see you again Ray, we should get together soon and hang out. Maybe go see a movie or something, Sandra suggested. Sure, we can do something, give me a call later this week and we can plan something, Raylynn replied.

Raylynn went straight home. She felt exhausted from the last few days. She got ready for bed and went into her room and just lay down on top of the covers for a minute. She just wanted to relax and was grateful that the day was finally over. She was so tired she just wanted to sleep. She crawled under the covers and closed her eyes and tried to think of beautiful places. She woke up early again the next morning. Turned her alarm off went to work and came home and worked on the time line for a while. She tried to stay focused but had a hard time trying to get the events in chronological order. She tried to keep the memories short and when a bad memory surfaced she tried to ignore the feelings that came with it. I just have to get through this, she thought.

Wednesday came and went; her meeting with Reverend Joe secmed distant and boring. She just couldn't enjoy anything in life these days. She wondered if life was going to be like this until she dies. She just didn't want to feel like this anymore. Feeling like she doesn't deserve to be happy. What did I do to deserve this? She thought as she finished with her time line. 12 pages of events in her life and more than half of them are bad unhappy events that weigh her down like lead bricks tied to her ankles. She felt like she was going to drown in her own emotion, sinking closer to the bottom with every memory.

Friday morning she could barely wake up to the persistent alarm clock buzzing in her ear. She reached over to the nightstand next to the bed and fumbled with the alarm clock until she shut off the alarm. She was so tired lately she could barely motivate herself to take a shower and get ready for work. 6:30 comes early when it takes forever to fall asleep she thought. She has been having trouble falling asleep because she just couldn't shake some of the memories from her mind. She went to work as usual and as usual she was five minutes early. Steve had her stocking shelves the first thing in the morning. She moved slowly and finally finished about noon. 1pm finally came and she was free to leave. Go home and get some rest Ray, you look horrible. I need my employees rested and happy, Steve said.

Raylynn went home and laid down for awhile and just tried to relax. She couldn't fall asleep so she laid there and just thought about the time line and what she wanted to talk about at her appointment today. About 2:30 she got up and got ready to go to her appointment. She gathered her things and her time line to make it easier to leave when Reverend Joe arrived to pick her up. She made a fresh pot of coffee and just sat at her dining table sipping her coffee waiting for Joe. He arrived a few minutes early and she was thankful that she was ready. She invited him in and offered him a cup of coffee which he gladly accepted. Thanks Ray, I was running out of steam and really needed a cup of coffee. He said as he picked up his cup. No problem Joe, I needed a cup of coffee myself she said with a grin.

Do you have your time line ready? He asked. Of course I do Joe, she said with confidence. I always do what I am supposed to do. He smiled and said, that's good Ray, I like to see that you are on top of things. They finished their cup of coffee and were on their way to the clinic. The clinic is only 15 minutes away from Raylynn's place then they arrived a few minutes early. Raylynn checked in as Reverend Joe sat down. Raylynn fumbled with the papers covered in her time line. She looked through them over and over as if she were going to find something new. Once she had checked in she walked over to where Reverend Joe was sitting and quietly sat next to him. Before too long Sara called her name. Raylynn got up and walked over to Sara who was smiling. As Raylynn moved closer Sara smiled and said hello.

How have you been doing this week, Sara asked politely. Fine I suppose Raylynn replied. They arrived at Sara's little office and Sara opened the door. Raylynn walked over to the table and sat down in her usual place. So, you have been doing good Raylynn? Sara asked. Well, I have been having trouble falling asleep at night and feeling a little stressed, she replied. Were you able to finish the time line? Sara asked knowing she had. Yes Raylynn replied as she handed her time line to Sara. Wow, you did a great job on this Raylynn, Very good. Looks like you were able to remember quite a bit. Let's take a look. Raylynn nodded. They looked over the time line. There were lots of events on her time line. There was a good side and a bad side. Tell me about this Raylynn, is this the side of all the good experiences and this is the bad experiences, she asked pointing to each side. Yes, Raylynn replied.

They talked about some of the issues Raylynn had with creating her time line. They discussed how it triggered memories that were not so nice and how in the beginning when she was very young her good memories seemed to nearly always trigger a bad memory as Raylynn sobbed. Sara told her that to remember things when we are younger than 4 or 5 years old it is usually because it is associated with a trauma of some sort. They didn't go over the time line in this visit but more over how creating the time line affected her. She told Sara about the nightmares and having difficulty sleeping.

Sara reminded her that the time line was to help her to understand Raylynn and that this would not necessarily help her heal. It will simply help Sara become more familiar with her life experiences and help her understand her more. Raylynn nodded in agreement that she understood. That's all the time we have today, Sara said as she closed the file on the table. Sara walked her out to the waiting room and they said good-bye. Joe got up and walked Raylynn out of the clinic and to the car. As he looked at her, he could tell that she had been crying.

How ya doin' Ray, he asked with concern. I'm fine she said as she got into the car. Would you like to go get a burger at Jim's Burgers, he asked softly. Not today Joe, but thank you. She replied. Okay, what would you like to do now, he asked as he smiled to cheer her up. She tried to grin as she told him that she just wanted to go home. Awwww why Ray? He asked disappointed in her answer. I'm just tired Joe, I would like to go home and relax for a while, She said. Are you okay Ray? He asked again with concern. Yep, I'm fine; I just want to go home, She replied with a serious expression. Okay Ray, I will take you home, He said. He sat quietly thinking about what could help her as he drove her home. As they pulled into the parking lot he asked her about Sandra. Did you see Sandra last Sunday, He asked. Yep, she replied. You should call her and make plans to go do something fun. Have a girl's night out ya know, he said cheerfully. Yeah, I will call her soon. We will go see a movie or something. Barbara was telling me about a movie she seen recently. It sounded pretty good so we might do that. She said trying to sound like nothing is bothering her.

He walked her to her door and said, Ray, if you need someone to talk to, I'm here for you. You can always call me anytime day or night, okay? He told her as he held her hands in his. Thank you Joe, but I'm fine, really, she said as she tried to smile. He smiled at her and said good night. He couldn't help but feel concerned about her as he walked back to the car. He turned and took one more look back at her as she walked into her apartment and closed the door.

Chapter 4

Hanging Out with an old Friend

Saturday morning Ray got up and went to work. Steve looked at her as if she were the bad child. He walked up behind her as she was stocking the shelves and said Raylynn can I talk to you for a minute in my office. Raylynn put the box of candy she was stocking down on the floor and walked with Steve to the back room. Steve looked at her and said Ray, I don't know what is going on with you but you look like you are sick or something. I think you should take a few days off. You need to get some rest. I don't have you scheduled again until Tuesday. I want you to take Monday off and do something fun. Go visit family or a friend. You seem so stressed out. Ray was a little relieved to have an extra day off and a little stressed as well because that means she will be 8 hours short on her next pay check. She nodded and said okay I will see what my friend Sandra is up to. I will try to get some rest in the meantime. Good, Steve said.

She finished her half day and went home. I guess I will give Sandra a call and see what she is up to, Raylynn thought out loud. She pulled out her cell phone and called Sandra. Hello? Sandra answered her phone. Hi Sandra, Raylynn began. Hi! What are you up to Ray? Sandra squealed. Well, I have been really busy ya know, but my boss gave me an extra day off this week.

I was wondering if you wanted to get together and hang out. Oh Ray, that would be perfect. Sunday my cousin is having a birthday party for her daughter who will be turning 13. Do you wanna come? It will be in the early afternoon at the park. If you want we can go get some dinner before church. It will be great we can spend the whole afternoon together.

Sounds great, Raylynn said as cheerfully as she could manage. It would be great to hang out for a while. You will like my cousin she is a real hoot! Sandra exclaimed. Okay, see you tomorrow. Do you want me to pick you up, Raylynn asked. Um, sure that would be perfect and I will kick you over some gas money too. Sandra said happily. Great, see you tomorrow, I will pick you up at 1pm is that okay, Raylynn asked. That will be perfect see you then, Sandra replied. They said good-bye and Raylynn sat her phone on the table next to her laptop.

That night Raylynn had a difficult time falling asleep again and she laid there in bed thinking about tomorrow. It should be fun hanging out with Sandra she thought. It has been a while since she has done anything really fun and it might be just what she needs, she thought as she drifted off to sleep. She woke up from another nightmare. This time it was a shadow creature chasing her. It was gaining on her and Raylynn woke up gasping for breath. She sighed and looked at the clock. It was 4am and she lay back down and tried to settle in enough to go back to sleep. It took her a few minutes but she was soon asleep once again. She slept in until 9am Sunday morning for the first time in the last few weeks. She finally felt a bit rested and was looking forward to the day ahead. She got in the shower singing her favorite songs she washed and got out. The day was already starting out on a good note and she was feeling a little more energetic than she has been lately.

She looked in the mirror and the dark puffy circles around her eyes were almost gone. She pulled her hair back and threw on her makeup. She put on a nice pair of slacks and blouse. She figured it would be okay to wear slacks to church for once. She went out to the kitchen and made her breakfast. She had apples and bananas for breakfast today and of course a strong cup of coffee. She remembered her meeting with Joe and thought she'd better call him and let him know she wouldn't be meeting with him today. She felt kind of bad about leaving him out today but she really needed some time with her friend.

She called Joe and told him her plans today and that she was sorry to call off their meeting. He said okay and he seemed fine with her bailing on him at the last minute and he said good-bye. Raylynn thought about how nice he seemed to not be upset about her calling off the meeting for the day.

She was soon on her way to pick up Sandra. She was so excited to finally get out and do something fun. A teenage girl's party ought to be fun she thought. Us adult women can hang out while the teens do whatever teens do for fun these days. She pulled up to Sandra's house and Sandra was on her way out the door already. Hi Sandra, Raylynn called to her through the car window. Hi, Ray, she answered back flapping her arms as if she were attempting to fly away. Are you ready for some crazy kid in the park fun Ray, she asked as she got into the car. Yep, I am all ready for some fun.

They arrived at the park in just a few minutes. Raylynn drove around the park looking for signs of the party. There it is! Exclaimed Sandra as they approached what looked like a group of young girls tying balloons to the picnic benches. Raylynn parked nearby so that she could keep an eye on her car. Hi girls, Sandra squawked as they got closer to the group. Where is Missy? Sandra asked one of the girls. Her mom is going to bring her, she should be here soon one of the girls replied. Missy is my cousin's daughter, the birthday girl, Sandra said to Raylynn as they walked around the area. Looking good girls, you're doing a great job, Sandra said loudly for all the girls to hear. Sandra and Raylynn took a seat on the nearby grass under a large oak tree.

What a beautiful day, Raylynn said as she sat under the tree and looked around. Not too hot today, it is just perfect, Sandra added. They talked as they watched the girls decorate the area until Missy and Clara arrived. Come on Ray, I want to introduce you to my cousin. They ran over to greet the birthday girl and her mom. Need help with anything Clara? Sandra asked. Um, yeah, could you bring the bag of gifts from the trunk please? Sure thing, Sandra said as she headed toward the car. She reached in the driver's side and popped the trunk open. There was a full sized garbage bag full of gifts inside the trunk. She carefully lifted it out of the trunk. Need any help Sandra? Raylynn asked. Naw I got it, looks heavier than it is, Sandra replied as she carried the bag to the tables.

Sandra introduced Raylynn to Clara and they had a blast talking about the old days and the 80s. They played games with the girls and handed out prizes to the winners. The cake was amazingly moist with whipped cream frosting. It was a cake decorated with a photo of the birthday girl. Raylynn hadn't laughed that much in what seemed to be forever. It was good to get out and not have to worry about anything. She would have all day tomorrow to worry about stuff. After the party they went to Chums rotisserie chicken palace and had dinner. They sat down and picked up the menu. So, I hear you have been spending a lot of time with Reverend Joe lately, Sandra said teasingly. We are just friends Raylynn said as her face turned red with embarrassment. So what are the old gals saying about us? Raylynn asked. Oh, you know the usual, well that you two are secretly dating and they are trying to guess when you guys are going to break the news to the congregation.

Sheesh, those old women gossip so much. We are just friends. He is helping me with some stuff and that is it. Raylynn said. Well, I think you two would make a great couple Sandra added as she placed her menu on the table. I'm ready to order how about you Ray? She asked cheerfully. Um, yeah, I'm ready too.

After dinner they went straight to the church. Reverend Joe was just unlocking the doors as they pulled into the parking lot. Raylynn parked as close to the building as she could. They sat there for a minute to give Reverend Joe enough time to unlock the doors and begin setting things up. Sandra looked over at Raylynn and said I think he's cute. I can see you two getting married right here in the sanctuary she teased. Oh stop it! Raylynn exclaimed as she began to blush. You know I am not in the market to date right now Sandra, Raylynn said firmly. Oh come on Ray, you have been single for five years now. It's about time you found someone, she said.

Why does everyone keep trying to fix me up every time I turn around? Raylynn said with a sigh. They looked at each other and both giggled as they walked inside to see Reverend Joe standing on a chair with a broom in his hand. They both looked up at that moment and seen the big fat cat on the shelf to the right of the podium. Awww how did that get in here Sandra squawked with delight as she walked toward the cat. She walked right up to the cat and reached up, here kitty kitty, she called to the cat. The cat sniffed the air and jumped down from the shelf onto the floor and began to purr as it rubbed against Sandra's leg. What were you going to do Reverend Joe, hit the poor thing? Sandra asked as she picked up the fat cat. The cat was white with orange patches on the bulk of its body with big green eyes. It still had its claws and was wearing a collar with a little bell. It was licensed and had the name Tobias engraved on a metal personalized pet tag in the shape of a paw. Well, you can tell it's well fed, Raylynn said as she reached out to pet the cat. ...And friendly too, Sandra added as she carried it to the door.

It must have got in when one of the others locked up this afternoon after Mr. and Mrs. Harding's 50th Anniversary celebration, he said as he closed the door behind the cat that was now happily scampering off. Raylynn smiled as she reminded Sandra that Reverend Joe was highly allergic to cats. They began to help arrange the chairs and set up the altar with candles and incense. Good to see you two hanging out together again. Did you have a good day, Reverend Joe asked with a smile. Yep, we had a blast today Raylynn said cheerfully. It's good to see you happy Ray, he said as he placed the last chair. Yeah, I guess I just needed a girl's day. She replied. My cousin is a lot of fun. She could be a comedian if she wanted to be, Sandra chirped cheerfully.

More of the members began to arrive and Raylynn and Sandra made their way around the little groups as they arrived. Raylynn and Sandra were considered the socialites of the church. They knew everyone and everyone knew them. If they didn't know someone they made it a point to get to know them. Sandra pulled Raylynn around the room from member to member like she used to do when Raylynn first started attending the church. Reverend Joe became clergy shortly after Raylynn began attending the church. It was only a year and a half after his wife up and left him that he decided to volunteer at the church as Sunday and Wednesday night service leader.

The church has services several times a week all run by volunteers with a desire to be there for anyone who might need them. It has been said that everyone does what they do because they get something out of it. It was true for these clergy members at least because they got a sense of value out of helping others. They each had their own reasons for volunteering on their own time and working their schedules around it. The members of the church made donations but these only covered the cost of each service and expenses of the church to house them. Any maintenance and repairs were all done by volunteers who donated their time and money to help maintain the church property. It was a small community and all were welcome to any and all of the services that the church provided.

The little church of 200 members who met at various times of the week for support from others who are like minded is a friendly and close little community. There were quite a few activities that were provided some free and some requested a small donation to cover cost. Raylynn found that belonging to this little group helped her hold things together when life seemed to be falling apart and she liked being a part of something so positive.

After the service she visited with Sandra a little longer as they flitted around the group of members catching up on the latest news. Raylynn left in a good mood and had little trouble falling asleep that night. It was sometime during the night that she was awakened by a frightening nightmare. She was dreaming that a crazed killer was chasing after her. He had stolen her identity and was trying to kill her to finish her off. Everyone around them just watched as she ran for her life. She was scaling walls and chain link fences until the killer finally caught her. He was about to stab her when she woke up. Gasping for breath in a cold sweat she got up and went to the kitchen to get a glass of water. The window air conditioning unit kept her apartment comfortably cool in the summer but she was sweating nonetheless. It took a few minutes for her heart to stop beating so hard it felt like it was about to leap out of her chest.

She finally calmed down enough to try to go back to sleep and crawled into bed. She decided to leave the little night light on in case she woke up again. The next day she woke up just a little after 7am. She had the whole day to herself and wasn't quite sure what she was going to do with her time. Sandra would be at work until 5pm and Reverend Joe worked at the local library until 4pm then he volunteered at the local shelter for victims of domestic violence until 9:30 pm. She walked over to her computer and browsed the internet for the latest movies, listened to songs and checked out some videos. After lunch she decided to go to the library and see if she could find a book or two about dreams.

She managed to find a couple of books on dream interpretations and decided to browse through them over the next week and try to interpret her dreams. She was sure she could find something online but she loved the smell of books. She loved the smell of all the old books in the library and she especially loved the smell of the new freshly printed books in the book store. She buried her nose into one of the books and deeply inhaled the smell of the ink and paper. It reminded her of school when she was little. She loved school and especially loved it on library day. She could borrow a few books as long as they were for her grade level and she loved the wonderful little stories she would find. She often got lost in the little tales and the fun books that rhyme. She loved poetry and lovely short stories. She loved story time when the teacher would read little story books. Anything was better than being at home with her mother.

Her mother was not a bad person and she made sure she ate, was clean and that she brushed her teeth but Raylynn remembers all the times that her mother also pulled her hair or smacked her in the face when Raylynn didn't do what she was told fast enough or when she said the wrong thing. Most of all her mother always denied what her father was doing to her. She remembered her mother cleaning the bathroom when she was a small child and she told her mother what her father had done. Her mother hit her so hard in the mouth that it made her lip bleed. It made her mother so angry that Raylynn told on her father. It was a vivid memory almost like she was there in that bathroom all over again. Suddenly she was nearly knocked over when a woman bumped into her. The woman was very apologetic and seemed to be in a hurry as she went on her way.

Raylynn decided she had enough books picked out so she went to stand in line to check out the books on dreams she had found. She wanted to just get away from the memories. She just wished she didn't have to relive the memories like that. It is more than just being lost in thought; it is like she is being ripped through time to experience the event all over again. She hated that and wished these things never happened.

She checked out her books and went home. She wondered around her apartment a bit then decided to look through her borrowed books. Raylynn loved the smell of the books. They had such an old smell. She buried her nose in a book and inhaled the smell of the book once again. She remembered her favorite story as a child that a teacher had read to the class. It was about an old man who sat in the middle of a town and got all the citizens to contribute food that fed them all. What amazing adventures she had with all of those storybooks she read as a child and young teen. It has been a while since she has sat down and read a book just for fun. Usually it is to gather information and learn how to do something. She read mostly textbooks and reference material these days. She really needed to go on an adventure but she didn't know when she would ever have the time to just sit and read a tale about an adventure. Oh well, maybe someday when I get a vacation I will just lock myself up in my room and read for a whole week straight, she thought.

Wednesday finally got here and she met with Joe for their weekly coffee and sandwiches. They were sitting near a window at the coffee shop having an interesting conversation when Gerty walked through the front door. Reverend Joe said don't look now but Gerty is on the loose and I think she just spotted us. Raylynn looked over just in time to see Gerty moving toward them. Hello Reverend Joe and Raylynn she said cheerfully. Hi, Gerty they said in unison. What are you two young folks up to this afternoon and so close to service time too Reverend, she said with a smile. Ray and I were just having a sandwich and coffee, we were about to leave and head on over to the church, he said with a smile.

I'm just stopping in to get me a mocha Latte as a treat. I lost 3 lbs this week and I wanted to reward myself with something yummy, Gerty said. Raylynn congratulated her on her weight loss then excused herself. See you at church Raylynn Reverend Joe called out as she walked away. Raylynn looked back and waved with a smile at both the Reverend and Gerty. Gerty smiled and waved back as she watched Raylynn walk out the door.

She needed gas in her car so she stopped at the GoMart where she worked. She always purchased her gas at the GoMart because she was allotted a 20 percent discount on gasoline; one of the perks of the job. Wednesday night service was quick and sweet. Thursday went by quickly and Friday she found herself wondering what she should talk to Sara about at the appointment that afternoon. What will she have to talk about this time? She had no idea what to expect. I wonder if she has looked over the time line already, she thought as she finished her shift at the store.

She went home and changed her clothes, washed her face and hands, gathered her things to prepare for Reverend Joe's arrival. Joe arrived right on time and they were quickly on their way to the clinic. Well Ray, looks like you are doing well so far with the counseling. How do you feel about it? He asked. Well, it is still new and I still don't see how this is going to change anything for me, she replied. Well, he said. Ray you have to do the work to make things change and Sara is going to guide you. Essentially it won't change anything unless you help it change for you, he said kindly.

Raylynn thought about what he had said as they pulled into the parking lot of the clinic. While they were waiting for Sara to call her name, Raylynn looked over to Reverend Joe and said, Joe I know what you said is true but I don't know how to change these things. I just don't see how it's going to work. I will try to change things but it is so hard to deal with all the memories. I thought counseling was supposed to make things easier and yet it has only gotten more difficult, she explained.

Just as Reverend Joe was going to respond, Sara called her name. Just stick with it Ray, you will figure things out, you are a smart woman, you will see, he said as he patted her hand reassuringly. Raylynn smiled then walked over to meet with Sara. Once again they walked to her office. She walked in and sat at the table and waited for Sara to begin.

Sara sat down and began by asking Raylynn how she was feeling. Raylynn began by telling her about the dreams and the dream books she borrowed. She told her how the memories seem to come at the worst times and it was like she was reliving the experience all over again. Sara began explaining that when we experience a trauma that our bodies will record the trauma and kind of replays the event and our body will remember the event and that is why she experiences the flash backs. Raylynn understands memories but she still didn't quite understand why she felt like she was there all over again.

Sara wanted to go over the time line and talk about the first few events. Raylynn squirmed in her seat at the thought of talking about those earliest memories. Tell me about this one Sara said as she pointed to the first event on the time line. Raylynn looked to see the event playing with toys. Raylynn said, that is the earliest memory I have. I was sitting on the floor playing with my toys and my mother was sitting there. She was being nice and talking to me. Sara looked at it and said so this is a good memory, right? Raylynn said yes because I was exploring the facc of a doll and my mom was being nice. Oh okay so that is a good memory. Then you had your second birthday which was also a good memory, Sara said. Yes, I remember my mom and some other people kept asking me how old I was and I tried to put two fingers up, Raylynn said. Tell me about this next one, Sara said as she pointed to the event titled "molested in the car".

Raylynn frowned and squirmed in her seat again as she thought about that memory. She thought about what she was going to say. Well, she stammered. I remember I was little and I was wearing a little nightgown that went all the way to my feet. I was still in diapers I think. I kept tripping over my nightgown while I played with a ball. Every time I tried to pick it up I must have stepped on the edge of my clothes. My dad picked me up and said something to my mother and my mother smiled and said okay. My dad said we were going bye-bye. He took me out to the car and laid me down in the back seat of the car and took my diaper off. Raylynn cringed as she remembered the next part. He was doing something that hurt me down there and I remember crying. He wouldn't stop.

Raylynn began to cry, I don't know why he did those things to me. Sara listened quietly as Raylynn spoke. Raylynn looked at Sara and she seen that Sara didn't seem to be disgusted with her or appalled with her at all. She didn't seem to be judging her like she imagined she would be. When she was finished speaking Sara pointed to the next memory on the time line. I remember this little girl got hurt. There was blood everywhere. There was this man there and he was yelling and he scared me. When he came over to me, I cried loudly. It was a very scary event. Raylynn explained as she told the story.

Sara continued to listen quietly as they went through the time line events of chickenpox and measles and birthdays and the many moves all over the country. Then they came to the one event titled "told mom about dad". She went over the time that she and her mother were in the bathroom and she had told her about what daddy did to her and it made her hurt down there and how her mother smacked her in the mouth so hard it made her lip bleed. Raylynn went on to talk about the nightmares and how the bad dreams began and that she would wake up terrified and screaming in the middle of the night as a small child.

Sara looked at the clock and said I'm sorry Raylynn, this is all the time we have it's about time we wrap up and finish here. Raylynn nodded and settled back in her seat. She was relieved that she didn't have to talk about any more of these events. They looked at the time line in an overview at how many good things happened compared to the bad things that happened. They could see that there were more bad things than good ones. Sara concluded by stating, no wonder you have depression Raylynn. With all the things that have happened to you it would make anyone feel depressed. This made Raylynn feel like less of a freak and a little more "normal" like the average person. Although Raylynn was still upset about the things they had talked about she was feeling a little better about herself to think that she was like other people or that other people are like her. Sara closed the file and they walked to the waiting room. Raylynn said goodbye to Sara and walked toward Reverend Joe who was now standing.

As they walked toward the door, Reverend Joe asked her how she was doing. I'm fine, she replied after they walked out of the door. Raylynn got in the car and fastened her seat-belt. She looked over at Reverend Joe as he started the car and said, Ya know Joe, I never thought about myself as being like other people. I have always thought of myself as being the weird girl with lots of issues. I never thought that what made me different were my experiences and not my responses.

He just sat there and gave her a confused look. After a minute or so he took a deep breath and sighed. Did you really think you were weird Ray? He asked as he sat with his hands resting on the steering wheel. She was now the one with the puzzled look on her face. Well, yes, don't you think I am a bit weird? She asked. No, not at all Ray, he replied. He backed out of the parking space and they were on their way. I think we should go to Jim's burgers and get some dinner. I would like to talk to you about this a little more if you are up to it, he said. Sure, I don't mind, she said. I am a little hungry anyway.

They stopped at Jim's Burgers and went inside to place their order. Reverend Joe asked Raylynn what she wanted. Oh, I will have the bacon cheeseburger without the mayo and a frozen cola soft drink, she replied. He motioned toward the dining room and asked her to find them a seat. She loved Jim's Burgers because it was a nice little building with two sections. One section was the inside part of the diner and the other section was much smaller on the outer wall and it had lots of windows. No one was sitting in the smaller section which she figured would give them a little privacy and she could watch the cars go by.

She found her seat with a view of the main street and parking area. She got lost in thought as she watched the people come and go. She saw a young couple with two small children walking into the diner and wondered what their lives are like. The kids looked happy and relaxed although the parents seem to be very watchful of the little ones. They were two little girls one looked to be about 4 years old while the other seemed to be a toddler of maybe 2 years old. The father carried the youngest little girl and the mother was holding the hand of the 4 year old. As they walked into the diner, Raylynn could hear the little girl singing a song she remembered singing when she was in kindergarten. She was singing the itsy bitsy spider. Raylynn was taken back to kindergarten when she was learning how to do the spider with her hands. She remembered her teacher Miss Cindy singing the song in front of the class and the other classmates singing along with her.

Back then they went a full day with a nap time included when all the children lay on little rugs and took their nap. Some had rugs; some had blankets to lie on. Raylynn didn't have anything to lay on because her mother didn't send anything for her. She asked her mother if she could bring her little blanket to school to lie on at nap time and her mother became angry and told her she could lie on the classroom carpet and that would be good enough for her. Disappointed in the direction that her memory took her Raylynn looked around the restaurant to see Reverend Joe on his way over to their table with the tray of food and drinks.

He sat the tray on the table and smiled. MMM MMM this sure looks good, he said as he sat down. He had grown accustomed to Ray sitting close to the windows. Raylynn smiled and said, I love the food here. The burgers are so juicy and they are huge, I can never eat the whole thing. They each opened their burgers; Raylynn checked hers to make sure they didn't add any mayo. Satisfied with her order she took a big bite. So, what made you think about being or not being like everyone else? He asked just before taking another bite. Ray swallowed and said, Sara mentioned that with all the things that have happened to me in my lifetime that being depressed is normal considering all I have been through.

I never really thought about it before but I really have had more bad experiences than good experiences, she added before taking another bite of her burger. You are a smart, kind and normal woman Ray, he said softly. Always remember that, he said. Raylynn thought about what he said as they finished their dinner. They talked a bit about some of Raylynn's not so bad memories like school. He shared a few of his own. He told her about the little girl with glasses in Kindergarten that he was completely infatuated with. He was partial to girls with glasses all through school. Almost all of his high school girlfriends wore glasses. Raylynn enjoyed their conversation and she especially enjoyed the thought that she was "normal".

Chapter 5

The Boy in the Park

After the last visit with Sara, Raylynn began to wonder what her life would have been like if she had grown up with adopted parents who were kind and loving. What if they would have protected her from abuse? Would she have finished high school and gone to college early in life? Would she be happily married with a few children to care for if they were a normal family? She wasn't sure what her life would have been like but she enjoyed spending her free time daydreaming about it.

Wednesday was finally here. She woke up to her alarm bright and early after a strange dream. She dreamed she was in a big house and there were lots of people there. They were drinking alcohol and she was going to all of them and telling them not to drink and that there was church in the morning. She wasn't sure why she dreamed that. The church she went to did not condemn alcohol in moderation since wine was used in some ceremonies. No one was drunk in her dreams. She just figured it was left over fear from her past with past religious experiences as the emphasis in this dream.

Maybe she was feeling as though her life was about to spiral out of control and she wanted to keep things under control, she thought as she wondered about her dream. She thought of her borrowed books. It seems that to dream of alcohol means that you desire to escape a problem or that you are seeking pleasure. She thought for a minute and realized she was really wishing for happiness and fun in life but is afraid that somehow that would be a betrayal to her considering the church is associated to the divine and her fear of happiness was in some sort a betrayal of the divine. She also believed that the divine is within all of us and therefore the betrayal was to her. But why would she be afraid to be happy? She wondered. Then she realized that deep down she doesn't feel that she deserves to be happy.

She got ready for work and headed off to start the day. She got to work on time but was distracted all day with the whole concept of happiness. Why do I feel I don't deserve to be happy? She wondered as she dusted the shelves and cleaned up the soda machines.

4 o'clock finally struck and she was free to go. She hurriedly clocked out and grabbed her purse. Good night Steve she called out as she walked out the door of the GoMart. She drove home using the quickest route she knew. When she arrived at home and unlocked the door she seen Barbara walk up from the parking lot. Hi Barbara, Raylynn said as Barbara reached earshot. Hi Ray she said as she approached her. What you up to tonight Ray? She asked politely. Ray smiled and said, I am meeting a friend tonight. Oh? She remarked as if she didn't know. And what is his name? She asked with a smile. His name is Joe, he is just a friend; Raylynn then rolled her eyes and curled her lip. Is it the man who always comes and picks you up on Fridays? She asked. Yes, that is the one. Raylynn replied. Raylynn

knew she was just picking for information to gossip about. So how long will you two date before he is more than just a friend? She asked. Raylynn grinned and waved her hand as if to dismiss the question. Good night Barbara she said as she stepped inside and closed the door behind her. She giggled as she thought about Barbara's questions.

She walked into her room and changed her clothes then went into the bathroom and washed her face and hands. She brushed her hair and put on make-up for a change. Usually she doesn't put on makeup except on special occasions. She often felt that maybe if she kept herself plain and unattractive she will not be bothered by men any more. For some reason she just felt like putting on makeup for church tonight and wanted to feel pretty for a change. She hurried out the door to meet with Joe at their favorite place, the Dark Roast Coffee House. She had grown fond of the Ham and cheese sandwiches and coffee on Wednesday nights. She never thought she would ever look forward to hanging out with a man ever again but Reverend Joe was comfortable and understanding. He was turning out to be a pretty good friend. He was easy to talk to and had a good sense of humor.

She arrived at the Coffee House a couple of minutes early. She stopped to look for her lip gloss. She hated how chapped her lips would get if she didn't use it. Just as she found it Reverend Joe knocked on her car window scaring her half to death. As she jumped she dropped her lip gloss on the floor beneath her feet. She opened the car door and got out of the car. She frowned at Reverend Joe as she stated that he frightened her. She bent over and reached inside the car to retrieve the lip gloss. As she stood up Reverend Joe seemed a little uncomfortable. What is it Joe? What's the matter? She said as she applied the lip gloss to her slightly chapped lips. Nothing, why would you think something is wrong? He asked. Oh never mind she said and she headed for the door.

They walked inside and Reverend Joe asked her to pick a seat while he placed their order. Of course Raylynn's favorite seat was available and she quickly grabbed her favorite chair. It was still daylight outside and she watched people pass in the parking lot and on the street going about their business. Reverend Joe brought the two cups of coffee and sat them on the table then emptied his pocket of the cream and sugar. Raylynn watched him empty his pocket then sit down. She began to add the cream and sugar to her coffee in silence. Reverend Joe watched her for a minute and then said, Ray, you look very nice tonight. You look good with makeup. Why don't you wear it more often? He asked as he stirred the cream into his coffee. I got off a little early she said and I don't usually have the time or motivation to wear makeup. Besides, if I am not careful it will break out my face. She said as she took a sip of her coffee. Their visit went the same as usual. They chatted about the lesson he was going to give that night, they discussed work and what was new at the shelter.

She caught him looking at her strangely a couple of times but wasn't sure what it meant. Is something bothering you Joe? No, why do you keep asking me that Ray? He said as he wiped the crumbs from his sandwich off the table. I keep getting this weird vibe from you, like something is wrong. She said with concern. Nothing is wrong Ray, honest, he said earnestly. Okay Joe, I'll take your word for it, she said. Maybe it's the makeup she thought. Maybe it is throwing him off and I shouldn't wear it. No one is used to me wearing it. She began to feel self conscious. Well, I better get going he said as he picked up all the trash from the table. Are you done with your coffee Ray? He asked as he stood up. Naw she replied, I'm going to take it with me. Okay he said and off to the trashcan he went. She got up and met him near the door. He walked her to her car. She opened the door and got in. Just before he closed the car door he told her he would see her at church and to not be late. She giggled then said, I have to stop for gas, I will be there as soon as I can.

The Wednesday night service was nice and Sandra was there to drag Raylynn around to the little groups to say their hello and good-byes and catch up on the latest gossip. Raylynn went home feeling tired yet refreshed. It was as if she had gotten a breath of fresh air. She always felt like a kid again when she flitted around with Sandra. If for no other reason, Sandra was the breath of fresh air that kept Raylynn sane. Sandra was funny and she always teased in the right way to make everyone laugh including the one she was teasing.

She went home and got ready for bed. She was feeling a bit tired and was ready to just lie down. As she lay in bed waiting for sleep to take her into dreamland she allowed her mind to wonder about what life would have been like if she would have had a normal childhood. Before she knew it she drifted off to sleep. Sometime in the wee hours of the morning she woke up from a horrible nightmare. She got up and turned on the nightlight and went to the kitchen to get a drink of water. She sat in the living room for a few minutes while she drank some water and thought about her dream. Why am I having these dreams all the time? Why can't I just sleep through the night like a normal person? She asked herself. She walked back to her room and left the nightlight on and lay down. It took a few minutes before she could fall back to sleep. I should start with a new dream now that I sat up for a minute she told herself as she drifted back to sleep.

Thursday went by slowly but she managed to keep a positive outlook on life. Thursday night she got ready for bed but she left the night light on in the hallway just in case she was awakened by another nightmare. The nightlight was a soft light that lit up the hallway and the living room giving off enough light to make it easy to see the path to the kitchen. She closed her bedroom door to only let a little light shine from under the door. A soft glow was all that crept through. It was just enough light for her to make out the shape of the bedroom furniture and stuffed animals on the rocking chair across from her bed. Some of the stuffed animals were hers from when she was a little girl. She would pile them around her bed at night so they could protect her from the meat eater monster that lived in her closet.

They were her favorites and made her feel safe as she drifted off to sleep.

She was walking through a house. It was a house she used to live in when she was about four years old. She climbed up onto the toilet because she had to pee. Seemed so ordinary like an everyday event. She was sitting on the toilet when her father walked in the bathroom. He had that look on his face, the look of determination as he looked down at her. He wasn't smiling and she knew why he was there. She threw her little hand up at him in protest and began to cry No, No, No as he walked over to her. Kicking her feet and holding her hand up in protest he walked over to her and grabbed her little four year old wrist and began to lift her off the toilet. She felt this sharp pain in her underarm and shoulder as he lifted her. Suddenly she sat up in bed gasping for breath. Another memory coming out in her dreams for her to relive not only during the flashbacks of her waking hours but now taking place in her dreams as well.

She began to cry. She sat there in bed and just sobbed for about 20 minutes as the rest of the memory filled her mind with flashes of what happened next. Nobody stopped him from hurting her; no one stopped him from doing the things he did to her. Nobody cared. Her mother didn't want to hear about what her daddy did to her and her mother lied to others and told them she made up stories so they wouldn't believe her when she tried to tell someone else about what he did to her in the bathroom during the day and in the bedroom in the middle of the night. No one believed her when she told. She had nightmares ever since she could remember. She was afraid of the dark and was terrified every night as she went to sleep. She always begged to keep the hall light on and woke up screaming from the night terrors almost every night. She slept with a nightlight on every night as she was growing up until she moved out into her own place and then she always had a small night light on in the hallway in case she woke up in the middle of the night. The nightmares never stopped and the terrifying dreams of crazy men and demons chasing her along with the memories she relived through the nights and the days would often take their toll on her and she was usually left feeling tired and fatigued during her waking hours. On the rare nights when she slept the whole night through without having any bad dreams were her good days.

Why did she have to go through these things she wondered as she struggled to relax and fall back to sleep. She tried to change her thoughts to something nice. She tried to focus on nice places, her safe place where she is safe from anyone hurting her. She tried to imagine the water surrounding her and the warmth of the sun enveloping her body while the rays of the sun brightened her surroundings so she could run and play in the grass and under the trees. She tried to imagine the smells of the outdoors and the sounds of the birds and other little creatures scurrying about. She looked over at the clock and it was 4am. In just two and a half hours she would have to get up and get ready for work. It is Friday, a half day and the day she meets with Sara.

She finally drifts off to sleep only to awaken to the loud buzzing of the alarm clock. She feels exhausted but she climbs out of bed nonetheless. She gets in the shower and just stands there allowing the warm water run over her tired body. She washed her body and her hair and got out. She got dressed, brushed her hair and her teeth. She felt so mechanical like she was a machine just going through the motions of life. She washed her fruit and made a slice of whole wheat toast and butter. She ate her breakfast drank her coffee and went to work.

At work, Steve hovered over her like she was a two year old. He watched her every move. As he looked at her, he could tell that something was bothering her but it was none of his business. A couple of hours into her shift during a moment where there were no customers in the store, Steve looked at her and said, I don't know what is bothering you Raylynn but at least try to smile as you go through the motions so people at least think you like your job. Raylynn looked at him and sighed. I'm sorry, she said, I didn't sleep well last night. Yeah you are looking a little ragged, he said. Do you want to talk about it? He asked. No, there is nothing to talk about, I just woke up at 4 this morning and had a hard time falling back to sleep. She said without emotion the best she could.

Every Time she thought about the dream she wanted to cry. It was one of the most vivid of all the memories and the pain seemed so real. Her shift finally came to an end and she hurried to clock out and leave. Goodbye Steve! She shouted back as she ran out the door to her car. I thought this day would never end she thought as she got into her car. She drove home and went inside. She plopped onto the sofa let out a big sigh of relief. I am so glad to be home she thought as she sat on the sofa for a few minutes. I just need to relax a minute and then I'll go make some coffee she said out loud as she rubbed her feet.

A few minutes later she made her way into the kitchen to make some coffee. Her faithful little 10 cup coffee pot has lasted her for 3 years of hard use. She made just a half of a pot this time because she didn't want to drink a whole pot and be kept awake all night. She walked into her room and changed her clothes and let her hair down. She walked into the bathroom and brushed her hair, washed her face and hands then went back out to the kitchen to get her cup of coffee. She sat at the kitchen table and just relaxed as she drank herself awake. I just need a second wind she thought as she rubbed her eyes.

She put on her shoes and made herself a second cup of coffee just in time to hear Reverend Joe knock on the door. She opened the door and there he stood gleaming with sheer happiness. She invited him inside. Why are you so happy Joe? She asked after he stepped inside. One of the residents at the shelter that I have been helping lately made the biggest accomplishment. She pulled herself out of the depths of despair and right up on to the success train. Not only did she conquer her fears but she just landed a job as a supervisor of a very prominent company. I am so happy for her. I have been working with her for the last year. Oh, who is she. It's confidential he replied with a frown. But I am so happy for her. It has been a long battle for her but she did it. She went from being homeless, living on the streets to living in the shelter to a great job. She will be getting her own place in a month and that will open a spot for someone else for us to try to help.

Not all the people who find themselves in the shelter are successful and some even fall back into drug or alcohol abuse. She is one of our success stories and I am going to ask her if she will speak to the other residents in the meeting next Thursday night. She can tell them how she did it. He was brimming with excitement as he spoke. That is great news Joe, she said calmly with a grin. Do you want a cup of coffee? I have an extra to-go mug if you want to bring it with you. Sure Ray that would be great! He replied. She poured his coffee into her extra to-go mug and handed it to him. The cream and sugar is on the table she told him as she pointed in the general direction of her kitchen table. I will grab my things and we can be on our way she said as she ran off and left him to fix his coffee the way he likes it.

They were on their way in no time. He chattered the whole ride there about how rewarding volunteering at the shelter was and how hard it is at times but it was well worth the difficulties in the end. Raylynn just stared out the window and got lost in thought until they arrived at the clinic. She got out of the car and walked into the clinic. Reverend Joe was walking with the usual bounce in his step as they walked inside. She checked in and he went and found seats for them. It was evident that Reverend Joe was having a great day. He sat there with a smile on his face and his hands in his lap. Before long Sara called Raylynn's name and she was off to the dreaded meeting.

They walked back to her office and Sara opened the door. Raylynn walked in and sat in her usual spot. How have you been this week Raylynn? Sara asked as she sat down. Same as usual, she replied. I am so tired I can hardly think and the dreams keep me awake throughout the night. I had a new memory come out in my dream. It was very short but when I awoke I remembered everything, She said in a low tone. Do you want to talk about it? Sara asked politely. Raylynn began to tell her about the dream. She told her about her father coming into the bathroom and how she protested. She told her that he grabbed her and lifted her off the toilet and it caused pain in her arm. The pain in her arm and shoulder stopped when she woke up but the fear carried on for a minute or two. She told how she cried for a while and had a difficult time falling back to sleep.

How old do you think you were when this happened? Sara asked. About 4 years old, she replied. Sara looked down at the time line. Do you think it was before you told your mother about what your father was doing to you? She asked. I don't know, I'm really not sure of the time line. It could have but I really don't know, Raylynn replied. I will make a little note right here on your time line Sara added as she wrote a note next to the event "told mom". Let's start off where we left off, she said. Okay Raylynn said as she looked down at the time line to see what was next. Singing in kindergarten was next on the list. Let's talk about this one, Sara said. It's on the good side. You liked school is that right? Oh yes, I loved school. I always had so much fun there and I loved learning new things.

They talked about school and the next few events on the list. Then it went to the boy in the park. When they came to this one Raylynn cringed. Sara said this one is on the bad side, can you tell me what happened with the boy? Raylynn looked down at her hands and began to tell the story in a low tone. I was at the park and I was running past the restrooms when this older boy grabbed me and pulled me into the boy's restroom. Do you remember how old you were? Sara asked. Um about 7 or 8 I guess, Raylynn replied. He pulled you into the boy's restroom and then what happened? Sara asked. Tears began to roll down Raylynn's cheeks as she quietly spoke the words, he tried to rape me. What did you do? Sara asked patiently. I began to cry and yell for help. She replied.

Did anyone hear you? Sara asked. Yes, the maintenance man came in and pulled him off of me and called the police. He made me wait with some lady until the police arrived, Raylynn said. Where were your parents at that time? They were at home, I had walked to the park with a neighbor kid and we were there to go swimming in the little wading pool the park provided for us little kids. The park was right down the street from our house so it wasn't very far. It was a busy park. Of course this was back in the early 70s. We didn't hear too much about kids being kidnapped or bad things happening to children. A few weeks later the boy found me in the park and began to chase me with a knife. I had seen him stab the maintenance man who was trying to help me once again. If it is alright I would like to come back to that some other time.

Raylynn wiped the tears from her eyes and cheeks as they continued down the time line. They talked about the death of her hamster Benny and her cousin's death, they talked about a few more events then they came to the rape when she was a young teenager. Before they got into this event Sara stopped her there and said, we should wait for this one let's save this one for next time. She smiled at Raylynn and added I think we need to schedule the next few appointments, it shouldn't take too long. How are you doing with the appointment times we have had scheduled in the past, is the times working out for you? Raylynn nodded and said that she would like to keep the same schedule. They scheduled the next four visits every Friday afternoon at 4pm. Raylynn stood up and straightened her clothes. She looked at Sara who was now getting ready to walk her out to the waiting area. She took a deep breath and walked out of the room.

She said goodbye to Sara and walked toward Joe who was now standing. He caught eyes with her and smiled. She tried to smile back then they walked out of the clinic and got in his car. How ya doing after all this? He asked as they headed out of the parking lot. I'm doing alright I guess, she replied with uncertainty. That doesn't sound too convincing, he said. You wanna stop at Jim's and grab some food before I take you home? He asked as he looked at her with his puppy dog eyes.

She grinned and said no thanks, not tonight. Maybe another time, she replied. She just wasn't in the mood for company. She had a lot on her mind and wasn't ready to share that kind of stuff with him. She didn't think it would be that hard to talk about the boy in the park. It happened so long ago. She didn't even know she was that bothered by it until today.

When she made the time line it was one of the things she felt the least about. She had no idea she would be so upset when she said it out loud for someone else to hear. It was like a secret she never spoke about. She doesn't even know what happened after that because she never heard. All she knew is the boy came after her a few weeks later. He and one of his friends chased her through the park but she doesn't remember seeing him again after that. Her memory after that was vague and she couldn't remember much else.

Ray! Reverend Joe called her name. Raylynn looked up at him, huh? She said as she realized she had gotten lost in thought again. I'm sorry Joe; I just haven't been getting much sleep lately. I understand Ray, he said softly as he pulled into the parking lot of her apartment. Here we are, you're home. Would like to talk for a minute? He asked. No Joe, I have talked enough today. She said. Ray, it really will get better, you will see, He said to encourage her to stick with it. I know Joe, I know, she said with a sigh. He walked her to her door and they said good night. Joe walked back to his car and just sat there for a moment then he drove off. She walked into the kitchen and rinsed the coffee pot and got it ready to make coffee in the morning. She had another half day tomorrow so it meant she had to get up early again. She wished she could take tomorrow off. She really didn't feel like going in to work for a half day. Maybe I should call Steve and tell him I am not going to make it tomorrow and call off sick.

He should understand and I haven't called off sick at all yet this year. It's only a half day she told herself. She pulled out her cell phone and scrolled through the S list. Steve was the 5th one down. She finally called him. He picked up on the third ring. Hello, this is Steve. He sounded so professional all the time. Hi Steve, this is Raylynn. Hi Ray what's up? He asked. I'm not feeling very well and I need to take tomorrow off. I think I am coming down with something, she said as convincingly as she could. Sure Ray, no problem I will see if one of the other cashiers can come in and cover for you, he said reassuringly. Don't worry Ray, get some rest. I will see you Monday. Thanks Steve she said then she heard him hang up the phone. She sat her phone on the table and walked to the living room and sat down on the sofa. She took off her shoes and took a deep breath and held it for just a second then let it out.

I just need to relax and get my mind off of stuff so she went into her room and put on her pajamas and sat down to her computer. She decided to check out what her friends were up to. I think I will waste some time with a little social media and then check out what is on the television tonight, she thought as she logged in. After a few minutes her stomach began to growl with hunger. She looked at the clock, it was almost 6. I guess

I should eat something she thought and went to the fridge and pulled out some lunch meat. She made a sandwich and looked to see what was on television. She didn't watch television very often only when old movies were going to be on that she wanted to watch. She didn't see anything she wanted to watch so she went to her room and grabbed one of the books on dreams. She read until she was sleepy then got ready for bed. She left the night light on again. She has been doing that a lot lately. Then she laid down and snuggled in bed with one of her old favorite dolls.

Once again Raylynn was being chased by a crazy man who threatened to kill her with the knife in his hand. She was running through some trees and there was a fence. She turned to see the man chasing her as she got closer to the fence. Just as he was catching up to her she woke up. She sat straight up in bed as she gasped for air. She was so tired of having similar dreams of running from the killer who was usually chasing her with a sharp object. Why does she always dream that a killer is chasing her? Always a crazy killer. She got up and went to the kitchen and got herself a drink of water. She looked at the clock. It was 2am. She walked over to the sofa and sat down for a minute while she sipped at her water. She looked down at the coffee table and there were those books on dreams. She picked one up and was looking through it but she didn't find any suitable answers in it.

She decided to go browse the bookstore tomorrow and see if she can find something that will give her answers. If she finds something and it is too expensive she can always see if the library has a copy she can borrow. She has to return these books soon anyway. She thought about the boy in the park. She remembered how the Maintenance man stopped the boy from chasing her one day. He was going to kill her but the man stopped him from getting her. She was so young and the boy was so mean. He and his friends chased Raylynn all over the back area around ballpark. There was going to be an event that night and the Man was getting things ready for it. He seen the boy chasing her and stepped in front of little Raylynn.

She remembered the nice man's face as he told the boys to leave her alone. There was some shouting and the biggest boy lunged at the man and the man fell to the ground. Raylynn remembered the red stain in the man's lower abdomen and that he had been stabbed. She remembered running and trying to get help for the man. She ran up to a couple in the park and told them about the man who is laying on the ground and the mean boys. She never knew what happened to the man after that day. She had no idea if he lived or died. Only that he gave her time to escape and run for help. The man didn't believe her at first but the woman made him go check it out. Another woman came and took Raylynn home. Raylynn's memory of the incident stopped there. She could not remember any more of it. That was the last time she had seen or heard from the boy or the man. The park had been closed for a while and then Raylynn's family moved just a few months later.

She got up and put her glass in the kitchen sink and went back to bed. She was awakened by killers chasing her a couple more times that night. The next day she got up about 9am and walked out to the kitchen. She made a pot of coffee and sat down. She looked through the books one more time looking for answers and found nothing. It didn't make any sense that she would be plagued most every night with crazy killer men chasing her only to wake up as they are about to catch her. She got her cup of coffee and sat in silent thought. She was so tired and just wanted to feel fully awake then she would get ready to go to the bookstore.

She meandered around her apartment for awhile and flipped through the channels on the television. Finding nothing on television that interested her, she decided to take her shower and get ready for the day. After her breakfast of Berries and whipped cream with a slice of lightly buttered toast she gathered her purse and keys and took a drive to the bookstore. She went through all the books in the dreams section then decided to look in the psychology section. There had to be something in that section that would help her with these stupid dreams that torment her night after night.

After about an hour of browsing the bookstore she found a couple of books that peaked her interest. They were books on Dream analysis. She thought she might find some answers in one of them so she took them over to the sitting area and sat down and skimmed through each of the books. They were expensive and she didn't have the money to purchase them so she wrote down the titles of the book and the authors name so she could look in the library for them. She stopped on her way to the library and bought a small cup of coffee then went to the library. She found one of the books at the library but it was at another location. She decided she could wait for it and placed her request for the book. It should only take a couple of days she thought. All she needed were some answers. She hoped that somehow these answers would miraculously make her bad dreams stop.

Chapter 6

Ups and Downs

The next few days went by quickly as Raylynn went about the daily routine of her usual week. It was after 3pm on Wednesday when she started to feel a twinge of anxiety again. What was it this time? She was accustomed to the anxiety attacks that usually followed a thought, sound, smell or something else that triggered them. Quite often they were such subtle triggers that she could not figurc out what it was at all. They would just come up and hit her suddenly. This time though she was remembering going to the little store around the corner from her house when she was a little girl and buying candy with her birthday money she got from aunt Betty that year. She held onto the money for some time. It was a whole dollar and she could buy at least 10 good pieces of candy. It was just a quick memory flashback and wasn't even anything bad. It was just a memory about candy.

Sometimes her memories gave no reason to inspire an anxiety attack but the attack would happen nonetheless. She took a deep breath and exhaled then repeated the breath two more times. It is not that difficult to control the small attacks but some of them are so bad that she feels like she is going to pass out and is forced to sit down before she falls flat on her face. This time it was mild. She was relieved when 4 o'clock came around. She was able to run off and go home. She got home about 4:30 just in time to clean up and change her clothes before she had to be on her way to meet with Reverend Joe. She looked at herself in the mirror and thought to herself that she is really looking rugged. She reminded herself of one of those old women who have had a hard life living on the prairie in their old log cabin.

She pulled her hair back and walked out locking the door behind her. Within minutes she was on her way to the Dark Roast Coffee House. She arrived in record time. Traffic was perfect and she made almost every green light. There was Reverend Joe waiting for her by the door. She got out of her car and walked up to him. Hi Joe, she said with a smile. Hi Ray, did you bring your appetite? He asked as he opened the door. They walked inside and he told her to find a seat and he would place their order. He always paid whenever they met or went out to eat. He wasn't a big spender but he was paying three times a week which impressed Raylynn. She never had a guy pay her way all of the time. Usually her dates wanted her to pay for them both and Joe wasn't even a date. Then she thought about it and wondered if it were a date would he want her to pay at least half of the time?

It was a pleasant visit although very short. Wednesdays usually were short because Joe had to unlock the church for services. Tonight she decided to just sit for a few minutes after Joe left. She was in no hurry to get to the church. Usually she was about 20 minutes early but tonight she didn't feel like the usual visiting. She still felt a bit tired and she needed to just relax. She walked up to the counter and purchased a vanilla latte as a little treat to help her relax. She liked it sweet so she added a little extra sugar and went and sat down. She watched the people go by as she stared out the window. Raylynn looked up just in time to see Rose and Gerty walking through the door. She put her head down hoping they didn't notice her.

Oh look it's Ray! She heard Rose squeal from behind her. Raylynn turned to look at them as they walked over to her. She smiled at them and said hello. Where is Reverend Joe? Gerty asked as if she were concerned. He had to go unlock the church, Raylynn replied in a low tone. Oh of course it must be getting close to that time. We had best get our coffee Rose said nicely. I will see you ladies at church Ray said as she stood up. Good night dear, Gerty said in response as she shook Raylynn's hand. Raylynn walked out as quickly as she could. She was hoping to have a few more minutes to herself before she had to leave. Raylynn stopped at the GoMart and filled her gas tank then went on to church. She sat in a corner and sipped her latte hoping no one would bother her. She could only guess what the gossip was going to be tonight. Reverend Joe stood her up or they had a fight or something silly along those lines.

Raylynn guessed that gossip was what made the world go round and for some it was all they had to feel connected to the world. Let them talk, she thought as she sat in her little corner. Sandra wasn't at church so Raylynn didn't have anyone to pull her around the church and make her visit with everyone although some of the regulars seen her sitting alone and had to stop by to say hello.

After a Church service, Reverend Joe rarely has time to talk to her so she usually leaves him to do what he does before he locks up when all the members have gone home. She decided to wait until most of the traffic has died down because she didn't want to fight the traffic in the parking lot. Some of the members were a little less careful than others and she didn't want to ding her cute little car. Her Fiero was old but it still worked and other than a few signs of wear and tear and minor scratches it was unmarked.

She wanted to have the car painted pink someday. She envisioned a pretty hot pink would look especially awesome for her little car. She never seemed to have any extra money to put away for special things like that and with her anxiety and flashbacks working a second job is less than imaginable. She finally got home about 9:30 that night. She was so tired she just wanted to rest a minute on the sofa. She was beginning to think that maybe she was never going to get over these anxiety attacks and just learning how to manage them is all she could do. She thought a minute and wondered if she could change the way she thinks or maybe come to terms with what has happened to her it will at least be easier to deal with. Something had to change and it had to be something from deep inside her that had to do the changing.

She shook it off as she took off her sensible shoes and walked to her room. She put on her pajamas and went to brush her teeth. She wondered why brushing her teeth triggered memories or even flashbacks on some occasions but not others. She had no idea why she had flashbacks at all. I wonder if it is my mind's own way of helping me deal with the past she wondered as she brushed her teeth. Maybe remembering a little at a time is what I need in order to move beyond the past she thought as she rinsed and placed her toothbrush in its holder. She walked out, got a drink of water and took her sleeping pill. Something has got to give she thought to herself. I can't take this much longer. I need some real sleep she thought.

Thursday was uneventful and boring and Sandra and Reverend Joe were both busy on those nights and she didn't have anything fun to do except browse the internet or read. She was still waiting for the book from the library so she went to bed early. Friday morning she woke up bright and early before her alarm clock with out any memorable dreams. She felt a bit more rested than usual and was happy that she didn't spend anytime on the sofa drinking water although she woke up rather thirsty. She went straight to the kitchen after her bathroom stop and made a pot of coffee. She had a few minutes extra this morning so she decided to sit and relax before getting ready for work.

Maybe I just need to go to bed early every night she thought for a second then shook her head as she remembered on many nights she went to bed early only to wake up a couple hours later from frightening dreams. Well, in any case she had counseling today and was likely to have to drudge up some horrible memory that she would just really like to forget and wipe from her mind and never have to deal with it. She knew what Reverend Joe had said to her was true. She knew she had to deal with the memories and events and put them in their place or live her life not knowing how to deal with the anxiety and bad dreams. She just wanted to be able to deal with the stress of it all and control the anxiety attacks.

She got her cup of coffee, sat at the table and sipped it slowly while she relaxed. She drank almost a pot of coffee before leaving for work and was all ready to conquer the day. Her work day went smoothly with no issues and she thought "for once I am having a normal day just like everyone else". One o'clock came around and Raylynn bounced cheerfully out of the door and was on her way home. She got home and made a fresh pot of coffee. She bounced into the bathroom and washed her face and hands and brushed her hair then floated into her room and changed her clothes. She felt light, like she was walking on a cloud because her day went so well. She walked out to the kitchen and poured herself a fresh cup of coffee and prepared it with the cream and sugar. She grabbed her cup and glided over to the kitchen table and sat down. She had plenty of time to put on makeup so she sat at the kitchen table and put on her makeup while she sipped her hot cup of coffee.

After she applied her makeup she sat at the table and looked out of the window watching life go by. People were all out and about going there or coming here from somewhere. She actually felt good for a change. She didn't have an anxiety attack today at all, not even once and there were no problems, everyone was happy and friendly at the store and it was just overall a beautiful day for Raylynn. She got lost in thought for a little while, and then Joe knocked on her door and brought her down from the clouds. She walked over and opened the door with a smile. Hi Joe, she chirped cheerfully. Come on in. Hi Ray, he replied with a smile. Would you like a cup of coffee to take with you, she asked politely. Sure Ray, I would love a cup of your delicious coffee, he replied. She fluttered to the kitchen to fix a to-go mug for him.

What has you bouncing around all happy like this Ray? He asked with a puzzled look on his face. Nothing, I just had a great day is all. Have you ever had one of those days where it seemed like nothing could go wrong? She asked. Sure I have those days he said with a chuckle. Well, I am glad you're having such a great day Ray. It is good to see you happy. You deserve to have a good day, he said firmly. She handed him the mug and grabbed her purse then out the door she went. Come on Joe it's time to leave. Don't want to be late, she said with a big smile.

They arrived at the clinic and Raylynn got out of the car. She looked at the little square building and remembered they were still going over the time line. She felt a twinge of anxiety as she thought about what they discussed last time. She couldn't remember what was on the time line but she knew that it wasn't all good. She started feeling a heaviness come over her like she was walking to her doom. She was going to have to face the stuff she really didn't want to think about today of all days. She walked inside and stood in line to check in. There were about four people ahead of her but she knew it would go fast as it usually did. She finally got through the line and checked in then went and sat next to Reverend Joe. What happened to that sunny disposition I seen a few minutes ago he asked as she sat down. She looked at him with a serious expression and told him, "I realized what I had to talk about today", she said solemnly. It's going to be okay Ray, you will see, he said in the most comforting tone he could manage as he squeezed her hand and gave her a reassuring look.

Raylynn sat there in silence until Sara called her name. They walked back to Sara's little office and went inside. How have you been this week Raylynn? She asked. Raylynn told her about the nightmares and how today had been a good day. She had no nightmares last night and no anxiety for most of the day. To be more specific, she didn't experience any until she arrived at the clinic. Sara reassured her that they will be working on that later but for now let's just get through the time line she urged. Okay, she said as she nodded. Both now sitting, Raylynn watched her open the file. Let's take a look at your time line and see where we left off, she said as she pulled out the time line. Well tell me about this move? How old were you when you moved? Sara asked as she pointed to the next event on the time line. I was 15 years old. My mom got a better job and we moved into a bigger house. I see it is on the good side, so that is a good memory for you, right? She stated.

Yes, Raylynn replied. I loved that big house. I could listen to music and my mother didn't yell at me to turn it down. She would yell at me in the old house and I had to turn it down so low I could barely hear the radio.

She moved on to the next event. Set up by friend to be raped. What happened here, Sara asked. Raylynn shifted in her seat as she remembered that day. It was in the fall and my friend called me and asked if I could sneak out of the house later that night. She said there was a party and she wanted me to go with her. I told her I would try and she said she would have a friend with a car pick me up but I had to be out there by midnight. She insisted that it was going to be lots of fun. I snuck out that night and there was a guy in a car waiting out front for me. I walked toward the car and he called out are you Raylynn? I told him yes and he said he was there to pick me up. Sara interrupted to ask if he was alone. Yes, he was alone and he said my friend was at the party waiting for me to get there. We got to the house and the windows were dark and there were no cars around.

I asked him why the lights weren't on and he said it was in the back of the house that we had to be quiet so that we don't wake the neighbors. We went inside and he turned the light on. He told me to come to the back of the house he had to grab something from the room. He asked me if I wanted to smoke a joint. I told him no and he told me to have a seat in a chair in the little room. He offered me a drink I think it was orange juice mixed with vodka. I took it but I didn't like it so I didn't drink it. I asked him where everyone was and he said they would be there in a little while. Then He grabbed me and pushed me down on the bed. He tore my skirt as he pulled it up so he could rape me. I fought back and screamed but no one heard me. No one helped me. He had someone else take me home. It was an older man and on our way home he told me if I told anyone he would come kill me. I was only 15 years old when that happened and I was so afraid. Raylynn began to cry.

Sara waited and let Raylynn cry for a minute. What are you feeling right at this moment? she asked. I feel so helpless right now. I feel like I can't do anything to change my life and that people are just always going to do things like this to hurt me. Remember Raylynn, it isn't happening to you right now. It's in the past, it's just a memory. Raylynn grabbed a tissue and wiped away her tears. Let's move onto the next event. Tell me about this. You went to the prom? Who did you go with? Sara asked. I went to the prom with my boyfriend Tony. I was 16 and my mom let me buy a dress. We couldn't afford the beautiful ball gowns like the other girls wore but it was a pretty dress. I didn't usually wear dresses and this dress made me feel so feminine and regal. When he picked me up his mother had driven and she escorted us to the prom. I had a wonderful time. It was my very first real date. My mother didn't allow me to date until I was 16. I had my very first real kiss that night and Tony asked me to go steady while we were dancing to a slow song right there on the dance floor. It was held in a banquet hall and it was absolutely wonderful.

How long did you and Tony date? Sara asked. About 3 months, she replied. Yep three months then he moved away and I never heard from him again. I was so broken hearted. I cried myself to sleep every night for a month. Raylynn smiled at the thought that she once thought 3 months was such a long time when she was a teenager. I had such a different point of view on life and I was so idealistic when I was a kid, Raylynn added as Sara closed the file. Sara looked at Raylynn and smiled. She said, Raylynn have you ever meditated before or at least have an idea of what meditation is? She asked. Um yes, I have used meditation before. I still use cleansing breaths to help calm my anxiety attacks when they happen. She replied. That's good, Sara said. I would like to try meditation as we finish up, I think it will help relax you and lighten the anxiety for you. I know that some of the stuff we have been talking about is some really tough stuff and I can see that you have been feeling anxious.

I think it will really help and you can use it anytime you need to relax. Raylynn nodded and Sara turned down the lights and they sat in the dimly lit room while they took turns guiding the meditation. Raylynn imagined her sacred safe place with the waterfall and trees. She imagined the sounds of the birds and the smells of the grass, trees and shrubs around the wooded area. She really began to relax. They finished their meditation and Raylynn felt more relaxed than she had in a long time. She had forgotten about her meditations. She used to meditate all the time then she just stopped and eventually forgot about them.

They walked out to the waiting room where Joe was waiting and said their goodbyes. Raylynn walked over to Reverend Joe and said, let's get going as she smiled at him. He could almost swear he seen her eyes sparkle. Sure let's get out of here then, he replied with a grin. As they approached the car he looked over at her and she seemed more relaxed and happier than he had ever seen her leave the clinic before. They got in the car and buckled their seat-belts. Reverend Joe started the engine and looked over at her and said Ray, let's go grab something to eat. I want to talk to you about something. Sure! She squawked happily as they headed off to Jim's burgers.

Within a few minutes they pulled into the parking lot of the little restaurant. Raylynn still seemed to be cheerful. What gives Ray? He asked curiously. What do you mean? She replied. You seem happy like you just won the jackpot or something. Why are you so happy? He asked. I don't know exactly, she replied as they got out of the car. Well, what did you talk to Sara about? He asked. I talked to her about stuff on my time line. Some of it was bad and some of it not so bad. She said matter of fact. That made you happy? No, we did a meditation.

It brought back memories of when I did meditation with my meditation class and I had forgotten how good I feel after a few minutes of meditation. It really does work you know, She chirped happily. So that made a difference. Well, the meditation helped some but remember the meditation class was a big help. I remember the teacher of the class would always have us sit in a circle and she would burn incense and she would have this strange but relaxing music play in the background. She would always guide our meditations as she taught us how to meditate by ourselves. Then after class a couple of us girls would get together and go get a latte. That is a fond memory that I had forgotten about and doing the meditation in there with her reminded me of that. I don't know why I stopped meditating.

Raylynn was speaking a little fast as she went over the memory. Wow, he said with a little surprise. I had no idea that you ever meditated. He said with a grin. You know, I was told that it takes a lot of practice to meditate the right way. I was getting pretty good at it. He said proudly as he boasted about his meditation practices. We should start a meditation class at the church one day a week, she said excitedly as they waited in line to place their order. Oh not me, Reverend Joe exclaimed. I already have a lot on my plate. Maybe if you want to lead it you can volunteer for it yourself. He said. I can't lead a class she said. I haven't meditated in like forever. I don't think I would be any good at it.

The girl behind the counter motioned for them to step forward as she asked for their order. Reverend Joe looked at Raylynn and smiled then said, go get us a table while I give our order. Raylynn nodded and bounced off to find a table next to a window. The little area on the outside of the wall virtually empty and her favorite spot was free. She happily sat down and looked over at Joe and watched him as he carried the tray with the burgers and two frozen colas. He sat the tray down on the table and Raylynn seen he had purchased two slices of apple pie. What's the occasion? She asked. Just wanted to celebrate your first happy counseling session ending, he said. There will be many more you know. Eventually even when it is bad, you will leave knowing you are going to be better. He reassured her.

I hope so, she said. He smiled at her then took a big bite of his burger. They sat and talked about her first date with Tony and how it was her very first date she had ever been on and how she went to the prom with him when she was only 16. He talked about his first girlfriend in High school and they both laughed and had a good time. After dinner he took her home and walked her to the door. He looked in her eyes and he could see the fire of happiness burning deep within her eyes. Raylynn, you are a beautiful person don't ever forget that. You deserve to be happy. He said quietly. She opened her door and said good night. He walked back to his car and she walked into her apartment. She thought about what he had said and thought, maybe I do. Maybe I do deserve to be happy.

She walked into the bedroom and sat on the bed and took off her shoes and put on her pajamas. She walked into the kitchen and fixed herself a cup of tea then walked back to the living room. Instead of immediately sitting on the sofa, she walked over to her book shelf and picked up her old book on meditation. She walked back over to the sofa and went through the book looking for pointers or reminders on how and when to meditate. She went to bed at 10pm and this time she left the night light turned off. She decided she wasn't going to anticipate having bad dreams any more and that she would turn on the hall light on her way to kitchen if she had one. She was determined to meditate before bed every night to calm her thoughts and feelings before lying down to go to sleep.

She slept well this time after this counseling session and woke up feeling like she had a new opportunity to make her life better.

Chapter 7

Volunteering and emotional baggage

She felt as though she had slept like this forever. She hasn't had any nightmares for the last five days or so and she was feeling rested and healthy. That was unusual for her because she always seemed to wake up at least once through the night trying to shake off a nightmare or two. The last 3 weeks with Sara have been okay, most of the stuff on her time line had been the not so bad stuff to talk about or at least nothing major. Just the same old stuff about the abuse at home which was nothing really big and with the meditation at the end she was able to recover nicely enough to pull herself together before leaving.

Her dreams seemed to be shifting as she talked to Sara about her time line events. Just saying them out loud for another person to hear and hearing it out loud seemed to be making a difference. She didn't know why that would make a difference. It is like having a heavy weight lifted off of her shoulders. It has been a secret all of these years. She never really talked about any of the details before. She told a friend that her father molested her and that she had been raped but she never really talked about it. She never really told the slightest detail as to what happened before and she never told about her mother. It was as if she didn't say it out loud then it never happened. As long as no one knew about it she never had to really come to terms with it.

She wondered if her nightmares were over for good and that she was free of them forever. It was Wednesday and she had a full day ahead of her. She got dressed and pulled her hair up then went to the kitchen and poured a cup of coffee. Once the cream and sugar were properly added she took her coffee to the living room to put on her shoes and relax for a minute while she drank her coffee. She thought about how it was working to change her dreams and wondered if the anxiety was now going to go away now that the dreams were changing. She has actually been having dreams that she confronted her parents and had power over the situation. She yelled at them and told them they were child abusing perverts who should be locked up. In her dream she was the one in control for a change. Instead of her reliving the experiences over again she was changing the out come in her dreams.

When she dreamed of monsters or demons she was defeating them instead of them getting her with their claws and dripping fangs. The once terrifying dreams of her struggles with the monsters and the crazy killers seemed to all be changing and she was the one with the power. She had the power to defeat them, well, at least for the last five days or so. She ate her breakfast. For the first time in a long time she actually enjoyed eating the fruit and cream and she added a little cinnamon to the toast to add a different flavor to her food. It was all different, the day seemed different. For once she truly felt as though there is actually a chance to be happy.

She didn't know how long it would take or what needed to be done but she knew that there was a chance for her to overcome the darkness of her heavy secrets that have been weighing her down all of this time.

She got to work a few minutes early. She was earlier than she had been over the last couple of months. As she walked in Steve smiled at her and said good morning. Raylynn cheerfully returned the greeting. She clocked in and walked to the front to stand behind the counter next to Steve. You look rested today, he said. Yep, and ready to work she chirped with a smile. Good to see you doing well. I was wondering about you for the last couple of months. I thought I was going to lose you there for a while. Well, I feel pretty good today, she replied. Good, whatever it is, keep it up, he said as he walked into the back to count the paper goods and back inventory.

She finished her day that afternoon and bounced out of the store like she was walking on clouds. She went home and got ready to meet with Reverend Joe. She arrived at the Coffee house right on time. Joe was waiting for her just inside. She walked in and seen him sitting at a table next to a window. On the table in front of him was two cups of coffee and two ham and cheese sandwiches. He looked up, caught eyes with her and smiled. She smiled back and walked toward him. As she got closer to him he said, I got our order for us already to give us a little more time to visit. She blushed at that and sat down with her head down. She didn't want him to see her flushed face.

You look like you have gotten some rest Ray. How have things been the last couple of days? He asked. I haven't had a nightmare in about five days, she replied. I have slept the whole night through for the last few days. She said with a grin. That's great Ray! I'm glad you have gotten some rest. I wanted to talk to you about something that is kind of important, he said with a serious expression. Um, okay, what is it, she replied. Well, you can say no if you don't want to, just keep that in mind okay Ray. He stammered. Okay, what is it Joe, just ask already, she said.

Okay Ray, here it goes. The clergy has been talking about next spring and they think it would be great to start a meditation class. Reverend Charlene is going to lead the class but she would like for you to help her with it. That means you will fill in for her when she can't make it and sometimes lead the guided meditations. You have a great voice for it Ray and you can learn a lot from Reverend Charlene. What do you say? I mean if you need to think about it, you have plenty of time, He blurted excitedly. Raylynn just sat there with a confused expression, not knowing what to say. After a few seconds Reverend Joe said, just think about it Ray. She agreed that she would consider helping out with the class. The thought made her nervous. She has been practicing her meditations and has continued to use her cleansing breaths to help calm the anxiety attacks. Well, I will seriously consider it Joe, she said sheepishly. Okay Ray that is all I can ask. He said with a grin. They spent the rest of the visit talking about the service that night and volunteering at the shelter.

You know Ray; you would be great at the shelter. Maybe after you are done with counseling you can consider volunteering one or two days a week at the shelter. The Women there could really benefit from you just being there to talk to. I mean you have been through a lot Ray and you understand what it is like, he said. Yeah, maybe, we will see how things go then. I think I have a ways to go yet Joe. Before they knew it, the time flew by and they had to rush off to get to the church. Raylynn had to stop for gas but she got there just in time to be greeted by Sandra. Hi, Ray she exclaimed as she ran up to Raylynn. Come with me, I saved our seats in the front that way you can be close to Reverend Joe as he talks. I heard he was going to be talking about helping others and how important it is for the community.

Oh, joy she said as she rolled her eyes. He gets these ideas from time to time that everyone needs to give back to their community, Raylynn whispered. Sandra said well, it's true; everyone who is capable should give something, even if it is just going to the senior center once a month and visiting with some seniors, Sandra said with conviction. Oh not you too, Raylynn sighed. I have nothing against volunteering but I honestly just can't volunteer right now. I am one of those people who need help right now, Raylynn whined. Well Ray we don't mean you have to if you can't right now. What is this about Ray? She asked. Oh it was just something he said this evening is all. Oh, I am sure he meant well. Yes and he didn't say I should right now just that later when I can the women would benefit from me being there at the shelter. Raylynn said solemnly.

I think he is right Ray. They would benefit from you being there. You are a good person and I think you have a lot to offer and I am sure he feels the same way, Sandra said quietly. Raylynn just sighed but didn't feel any better about it. The service began as usual with singing and giving thanks then Reverend Joe spoke about giving freely of ourselves to help others. He said it doesn't solve all the problems in the world but it makes a difference in someone's life. Sometimes just the small things make a huge difference. Just being there for someone to talk to, reading a book to someone who can't read or mowing someone's lawn who is not capable of doing it can make a difference.

There are lots of ways to give back. If it is all you have to give, how about giving a smile to the homeless man on the bench in the park. Raylynn began to understand what he meant. Just to give what you can, it doesn't have to be what she thought which was a lot of time and energy. She is kind to people all the time, like helping that man catch his dog last week or the time she helped the homeless lady pay for her sandwich. It is the little things that count the most.

She realized she had something she can give and who knows maybe later down the road of life she will be able to give more. She began to really see the wonderful man Reverend Joe is. His views are so beautiful and he walks his talk. He volunteers here at the church as well as the shelter and he still goes to work at a full time job. What a good man he is and he still finds time to help me and talk to me about my problems, she thought.

After the service, Sandra pulled her around to visit with each of the members and talk about how wonderful of a speech Reverend Joe gave on giving. Sandra Volunteers twice a month to work at the Kitchen to feed the homeless. She serves them their food and she does it happily. She is hoping that next year she will be able to volunteer once a week at least. The company she works for has been having her put in overtime this year but next year they may not need her to do that so she is thinking she could volunteer more of her spare time to help feed the homeless.

She got home about 9:45 and just sat down for a minute. She took off her shoes and rubbed her feet then went to the kitchen to pour herself some juice. She turned on her meditation music and lit a few candles then turned off the light. She took her deep cleansing breaths and went through her relaxation technique and tried to meditate but she couldn't stop thinking about what Joe had said at the Dark Roast. After about 30 minutes she gave up. She knew that she was just going to get frustrated and then not be able to fall asleep so she simply blew out the candles, turned on a light and got ready for bed.

She finally fell asleep sometime around 11pm. Her sleep was restless and she had a nightmare. Again she was being chased by a crazy killer with a knife only this time he was stealing her identity. She has had this dream before although she didn't understand it. The book on dreams she requested last month never came in and she just wanted to understand why she dreamed the way she did. She got up and went to the kitchen and grabbed a glass of water. Well, she thought, at least I had five days free of bad dreams.

Thursday went by slowly. She felt as though the day could not get any slower as she waited for the last 10 minutes to get off of work. Steve noticed her staring at the clock and told her to go ahead and take off. She looked at him and smiled and said thanks as she zoomed off to clock out. Bye Steve she shouted as she practically ran out the door. He just snickered to himself as he watched her pull out of the parking lot.

That night she had a horrible dream. She was in the kitchen and she was changing her clothes but then her dad tried to come into the kitchen while she was naked. She tried to close the door but then her mother came to the kitchen door and demanded that she open the door. Raylynn yelled at them both to go away she was changing her clothes but they busted the door in. They were both yelling at her as she stood there in her underwear. She was upset and couldn't understand why they both just wouldn't leave and let her get dressed. She started yelling at them to get the hell out of her kitchen or she was going to call the police. She woke up about 2am feeling very angry. She put her face in her pillow and just screamed as hard as she could and hit the bed with her fist.

How dare they do what they did to her! They don't deserve her love or her understanding she thought as she gritted her teeth and squinted her eyes. She got up and stomped to the kitchen to get a glass of water. She felt so angry she couldn't stand to think about it. She stood in the kitchen and drank her water. She got another glass of water and went to living room and sat on the sofa. She took a few cleansing breaths to calm down. She sat there finally calm enough to try to go back to sleep so she went back to bed. She got up in the morning feeling a little irritable. After she got her morning coffee she took a few minutes to meditate and get back to feeling more herself. She was better feeling depressed she thought as she considered the angry feelings she was having since her dream last night.

At least I didn't have mean thoughts about people before. She began to feel guilt with her anger because she had thoughts of making them suffer. Making all of those who hurt her suffer for what they have done, not just to her but to everyone they have hurt. She just wanted them to pay and she felt guilty for thinking it. She got angry at herself for not having compassion for them. They too have been through stuff of their own. Both of her parents had suffered at the hand of their parents. They both have also been abused and she should feel compassion for them but all she could feel was anger when she thought about them. She was angry because they had a choice and they chose to hurt her.

She didn't have children because of the anguish her parent put her through and she didn't think she could handle having them. She didn't think she could be a good parent since she didn't have good examples for parents. Barry was so abusive to her that she didn't want to bring children into that then Greg couldn't have children and he was not much better. She spent her life wishing she could have children but being afraid she wouldn't be a good mother, and for what? She thought. Just because of them. All of them! She tried to calm herself and to change her thoughts. She tried to put it out of her mind.

She went to work on time and was successful for the most part at putting those angry feelings aside but she couldn't help but feel on edge all day. One o'clock finally arrived and she clocked out and was on her way. She didn't want to think about it for now. She got home and made a half a pot of coffee, changed her clothes and washed her face and hands then waited for Joe to arrive. About 3:25 Joe knocked on the door. She opened the door and invited Joe inside. He noticed she looked a little upset. Her face was red and she was frowning. Hi Ray, What's bothering you and I can tell something is wrong he said. I just feel so angry right now. I had this dream last night that made me feel angry and I just can't seem to shake the feeling, she replied. Do you want to talk about it? He asked. No, I will talk to Sara about it, okay? She replied. Okay Ray, fair enough, he said. Would you like a cup of coffee? She asked as she poured herself another cup. Sure Ray but I might need your to-go mug again, he said as he walked into the kitchen. No problem, I will get it for you, she said as she smiled at him. He looked at her affectionately as he thought about how pretty she is with her long hair flowing around her weathered face with its subtle features. He thought about how life has worn on her but it just made her all the more attractive.

She looked up and seen him looking at her. What? She asked with a confused expression. Nothing, he said as he took the coffee out of her hand. She giggled and said "you are so weird Joe", then walked past him to grab her purse. We should probably be going, she said as she walked toward the door. She opened the door and motioned for him to go first. They walked out and she locked the door. They were on their way when Joe broke the silence with a question. Why are you single Ray? Have you dated anyone since your last boyfriend 5 years ago? He asked with a most serious expression mixed with a hint of compassion. I don't know, she said. I guess I just didn't want the hassle of falling in love just to be abused or destroyed. My judgment seems to be impaired and I always fall for the wrong kind of guy so I would rather just be alone than to go through that again, she explained.

Why do you ask? She questioned. I was just wondering, I mean you asked me before why I am single and I guess it got me thinking and wondering why you're not seeing anyone is all, he said in a low tone. Okay Joe that is fair, I'll give you that one. They pulled into the parking lot of the clinic. Are you ready for your counseling session? He asked kindly. Yeah, I guess so; I mean I guess I am ready to talk about more bad stuff. I think we will be going over the time line for a while since it's so long. She said. Besides I have been practicing my meditations and we will probably do a short meditation afterward too. I think I will be fine.

Glad to hear you say that Ray. I was worried for awhile that you would quit going.

They walked inside; Raylynn stood in line and Reverend Joe took a seat close to the door Sara usually opened to call Raylynn. He knew Raylynn's little quirks about where she liked to sit so he usually tried to pick the perfect spot where she would be most comfortable.

After checking in she walked over to Reverend Joe and sat next to him. Before too long Sara opened the door and called Raylynn back. They walked to Sara's little office and for a second Raylynn had some anxiety. Their light chatter on their way helped Raylynn feel more relaxed and didn't give much time to think about what they may be discussing today. They walked inside and Raylynn went over to her seat where she could see the door as usual. How has this last week been for you? Sara asked. Well, some nights are good and I have had a few bad dreams but overall it has been alright. They talked a little about the dreams and the anxiety. Raylynn mentioned Reverend Joe's proposal to assist with the meditation class. They talked for a minute about how Raylynn felt about it. Raylynn wasn't sure she could handle the job. She wasn't sure how well she could handle the stress that comes with the responsibility. She was a bit shy in groups and wasn't sure if she would do a good job or not.

Let's take a look at the time line. I would like to move on to the next event because we still have so much to go over. Sara said. Raylynn looked down at the time line and the next event was when Sherri and I got arrested. Oh yeah, Raylynn said. I remember the time me and my best friend at the time got arrested. We were 16 then and very rebellious. We both got arrested for shoplifting at one of the department stores in the local mall. It was horrendous. They strip searched us and the police carted us off to jail and called our parents. My parents were furious. We were not allowed to ever associate with each other again after that. My mother told me how bad I was and that I was a bad influence on my friends. I wasn't allowed to have friends for the rest of the school year, Raylynn said as she remembered that day.

I was very isolated and felt very lonely. I started to really believe that I was a bad person and that is why all these bad things happened to me. Why did you decide to shoplift? Sara asked. Just to see if we could get away with it I guess. We didn't really want the stupid lip gloss and makeup. Heck, I didn't even wear makeup back then. She said as she thought about that day with remorse. I think we wanted to get caught but we just didn't realize it at the time. She talked about the boy she met who would call her in the middle of the night and threaten to hurt her parents or Sherri if she didn't meet him. Raylynn went on about the fear she lived in for six months and it finally ended when the boy was arrested for armed robbery. He raped her a couple of times when she met with him but for the most part it was just costing her some valuable sleep. It was more about the fear and lack of sleep that he got off on. He seemed to like the control he had.

She went on talking about the time she got caught with her friend's cigarettes on her birthday. She was in school and her friend had forgotten her cigarettes at her house the night before so she put them in her purse and took them to school. We were in the girls bathroom and I had my purse open about to give them to her when a teacher walked in and caught me with the cigarettes. I had to serve Saturday detention that year. I didn't mind though because it got me away from the house. I didn't smoke but the other kids thought I was a tough girl because they believed I did. I made friends with some pretty unruly kids that year. I started hanging out behind the arcades with kids who were high on drugs and listening to rock music.

They were the rebellious kids and I was accepted by them. I was so lonely I didn't know what to do with myself. I just wanted some friends, She said as the tears rolled down her cheeks. I met Barry that year. We were both so rebellious that we didn't get together then. He made some stupid comment about one of my friends and I thought he was a big jerk. I had a real chip on my shoulder that year. They continued down the time line across the bad grades and getting in trouble at home. She told about how her mom called her a whore among other choice names. Her mom pulled her hair and smacked her often in public leaving her feeling humiliated and embarrassed.

They talked about the time she went to the arcade with one of her friends and her mother came and got her but smacker in the face and yelled at her for not being home when she wanted her home. She smacked me right in front of everyone, Raylynn said sadly. The next event was her 18th birthday. She didn't get a birthday party; she never got a party or even a cake with a birthday wish. She got kicked out of the house. She was graduating from high school that year but on her 18th birthday before she could graduate she was faced with finding a place of her own. She never got to graduate from high school. She had poor grades anyway what did it matter. She got a job at the corner store and found an apartment nearby.

It was a small studio apartment and she usually didn't have enough money left after rent and bills were paid to buy food so she went hungry most of the time. She had to drop out of school to get a full time minimum wage job. A few of her friends from school often visited her and brought her something to eat. There were times when a few would get together and make their own version of stone soup. No one could afford to purchase a full meal but some could afford to buy parts of a meal. Her friends worked part time jobs while going to school. Most of them misfits themselves but they were there for her and she often would not have eaten for days had it not been for her friends.

As she talked about the past crying some and smiling some she continued talking. The depression got worse. Barry was being a jerk and blaming me for his problems. He thought we should move in together and I should take care of him while he went to college since I was the drop out. I have had to deal with depression before but it was at its worst now. Between Barry telling me how much of a loser I was and how I have no value and didn't deserve to go to school and the memories of the abuse I was feeling pretty down and worthless. Barry and I broke up and went our separate ways for a while. Raylynn cried as she remembered the feelings of worthlessness and Barry's words that she was not attractive nor deserved to go to school.

I was 19, it was just after my birthday, Barry and I had just broke up and some of his friends came to my house in front of my friends and called me a slut. Said I was sleeping around and that I had a sexually transmitted disease. Syphilis I think they said. They told all of my friends to leave that I kicked out their friend so that I could sleep around and they should all get checked for Syphilis. My friends left, all of them. A couplc of them told me to call them in a couple of days. I was humiliated and I couldn't face my friends again after that so I tried to kill myself. I took a bunch of pills a friend of mine had left behind. He had gotten hurt and was prescribed these pain meds and he brought them with him. When they all left he forgot to grab them to take them with him.

I took all of them. I overdosed and I almost died that night. It was a difficult time for me, Raylynn explained. Did anyone do anything about it then? Sara asked. No, I was released from the hospital as soon as I was physically stable. No one addressed the depression or the suicide attempt. The Psychiatrist told my parents I should move back in with them and that I would be fine. It was left at that and within a few days I was all moved back in with my parents. My life seemed so unstable. I lost my job, my apartment and I was back in with the people who kicked me out just a year ago. My mother didn't want me there and my father couldn't wait to get his hands on me again. I woke up one night with my father trying to touch me and I had a knife that a friend of mine gave to me and I put that knife to his throat and told him if he ever touched me again I would slit his throat. He never tried to touch me again after that. I was kicked out shortly after.

Sara stopped her at that point and they did a quick meditation. Raylynn was relieved to do the meditation to give her a chance to pull herself together before she went back out to the waiting room. She knew not to wear makeup to the counseling sessions because tear streaked makeup is well known sign that a girl has been crying. She didn't want anyone to know she has been crying. Never let them see weakness, she thought as she walked out of the office. Reverend Joe stood up as he seen her walk through the door to the waiting room. Tough visit today Ray? He asked. Yeah, just a bit, is it that obvious? She replied. Well, I just know you and I can see the sadness in your eyes, he said as he squeezed her arm. They walked out and made their trip to Jim's burgers and had dinner on their way to Raylynn's apartment.

Chapter 8

A New Dress

The bad dreams, the anxiety, and the depression seemed to linger over the next two days. Sunday finally arrived and Raylynn could sleep in if she wanted to but she didn't sleep in too late. She was awakened by a crazy dream of horses and long roads. Horses were following her. The dream made no sense at all. She woke up feeling confused and very lonely. She felt as though she had lost something but couldn't place what it was. She got out of bed and got ready for the day. Her first stop was the bathroom. While in there she looked in the mirror at her reflection. She seemed to look so old and worn down. She reminded herself of the crazy professor with her hair all matted and askew. She brushed her hair but it didn't seem to help much. It just made her hair frizz up like she stuck her finger in a light socket.

She made her way out to the kitchen to make her a pot of coffee. She rarely drank the whole pot of coffee but almost always made a full pot nonetheless. Shc prepared her cup of coffee and sat down at the dining table in front of the window. She just looked outside and watched life go by. She watched the neighbors go about their business early on Sunday mornings. Mr. Jones was coming with a small bag of a few groceries. The couple across the way just opened their living room curtains and she could hear Barbara upstairs getting ready for her Sunday morning church service. Barbara went to church every Sunday morning. It was already 8:30 am and Raylynn was still in her pajamas. Sunday was her usual day off and she always lounged around in her pajamas until about 10am and she would get ready to meet with Joe.

She was really beginning to enjoy her time spent with Joe. Sandra was often busy and Raylynn didn't have very many friends. Spending time with Joe seemed to pick up her life a little. She was really beginning to like him. She even found him a bit attractive. She always did fall for the hero types. She thought about how different Joe was from all of the others guys she has been involved with and wondered if he would ever be interested in her more than just a damsel in distress or someone to save. He was always saving someone it seems. Although he was always helping others he never missed a meeting. He was late on a few occasions but he was never missing. He always seemed to have time for her no matter what. That made Raylynn feel like she was worth something to someone. He always made her feel special although she knew it wasn't in a romantic way, she felt special nonetheless.

She got lost in thought for a while until the family down the way walked past her window all dressed up in their Sunday best. She briefly flashed back to when she was a child and her mother was yelling at her to sit still while she ripped the brush through Raylynn's long curly hair pulling a handful of hair out as she did so.

Her mother complained about brushing her hair for her when she was old enough to do it herself. Raylynn was about 8 years old and she remembered her mother's words. I should cut off all of your hair like a boy. Then maybe you will learn how to take care of your hair yourself she snarled. Raylynn remembered the white dress with the blue ribbon belt she wore one Sunday a month. It was her favorite dress and she loved to wear the little tights to church. It made her feel like a big girl. She was grateful when her mother finally stopped brushing her hair for her when she was about 10 years old.

Raylynn got up and prepared her fruit and whipped cream with her single slice of buttered toast. She heard Whole wheat was better for the body so a few months ago she started buying it. She liked the flavor of it over the plain white bread her mother used to buy. She ate her breakfast and before she knew it, 10 am was already here. She got up and went to bathroom and stepped into the shower and got cleaned up. She left her long curly grey streaked hair hang down. She decided she was not going to pull it back today. She liked the way it fell around her face. It made her features more distinguishable and made her feel a little younger. She put on her only dress and looked in the mirror. It was beginning to look a bit worn out and old. She looked at the time and decided to balance her checkbook. She had $20 she could spend on whatever she wanted.

She looked at the clock and it was 11:30am. She still had time to go shopping. She went downtown to the local Gables Discount Department store. She browsed for a bit and made a few selections to try on. She didn't really like shopping and has always been quick about it. She went and tried on the dresses and made her selection. It was very professional; in fact it looked like something one would wear to an office. It was plain and very burgundy. She loved the color and the way it made her feel. It was only $16.99 plus tax. She made her purchase and went to the ladies room and changed clothes making sure to remove all of the tags. She took a look in the mirror and seen the lines on her face. Where have all the years gone she thought as she smoothed out the dress.

She had some time to get to the coffee house with a few minutes to spare. Before long she was on her way. She arrived a few minutes early and just sat in the car. She didn't like to wait inside for Reverend Joe. She felt uncomfortable sitting there all alone. She reached over for her purse and retrieved her lip gloss. Her lips were always so dry that she had to use the lip gloss to keep them from chapping. She put away her lip gloss just in time for Reverend Joe to walk up behind her and gently tap on her window. Glad to see him, she greeted him with a smile. He opened her door and helped her out of the car. Wow! He exclaimed. You look very nice. Is that a new dress? He asked, yes, do you like it? She replied. I think it is beautiful but what is the occasion? He asked. My dress was getting old and worn out and simply needed to be replaced, that's all. She said matter of fact. Well you look great. Let's get inside. I am starving and in desperate need for a cup of coffee, he said happily. They went inside and he motioned toward the tables by the window and said you go ahead and find us a seat, I'll place our order. Raylynn nodded with a smile and did just that. She found her usual place near the window and took a seat.

In no time He was at the table with two cups of coffee and a pocket full of cream and sugar. The order should be up soon, he said as he emptied his pocket. Good, I'm actually hungry today, Raylynn said while she rubbed her tummy. She chatted about her shopping spree as he sat back and watched her talk. He couldn't help but think how pretty she was when she was excited about something. He loved the way her eyes sparkled and danced as her hands flew everywhere. He loved her gestures and wondered how anyone could be so mean to her. His feelings for her were growing with every moment he spent with her. He knew she wasn't emotionally available for a relationship yet but with this time with this woman he wanted her to heal so he could ask her out. He wanted to see her become her full potential and become available for him. He knew she had the strength even if she didn't.

Are you even listening to me Joe? She asked as he stared at her. Yes Ray, I'm listening to you. I think you made the perfect choice. You look great in that dress, he said with a grin. I really do love this dress, she said as she placed her hands in her lap. Hey Ray, I want to go see what is playing at the movies. I haven't seen a movie in a long time and I can't exactly go alone. I was wondering if you wanted to hang out with me for a little while and go to the movies. We will go see what's playing. What do you say? He asked as he looked at her with those big brown puppy dog eyes. Um sure, I guess I can't let you go to the movies alone, she replied. Great! We can hurry with our meal and head on over to the theater.

They got to the theater and were deciding which movie to see. Oh, let's go see Haunted Ghost she said. I don't know if we should see a scary movie Ray, you already have bad dreams. Oh geeze, I am not a baby Joe, she said as she rolled her eyes. Besides I have you here to protect me and it isn't that scary. My neighbor Barbara was telling me about it last week. It's a bit creepy but not really all that scary. She said it was a good movie and I seen the trailer, it looks like it will be good. He looked at her as she gave him her most pleading expression. Oh, I guess, I like scary movies and I have to admit it did look good from the trailer. They went into the theater and found their seats about the middle where it was not too far away nor too close. They found the perfect seats. Do you want anything from the snack bar Ray? He asked. Um, no Joe we just ate silly, she giggled. Raylynn enjoyed the movie and it wasn't that scary just like Barbara said.

After the movie Joe drove her back to her car. I have to go unlock the church soon Ray. Thanks for going to the movies with me, he said as she opened her car door. Thank you for inviting me. I had a great time, she said as she looked into his eyes. She felt all warm inside and thought about how kind he is. Her affection for him was starting to grow a little every time she seen him. I'll see you later, he said with a grin. See ya later she replied then got in her car. She figured she was safe with Joe. He would never want to date her. He helps lots of women and never dates them. Of course she didn't stop to think about the fact that he never spent time with them like he does her.

Sandra was at church and they hung out together as usual. They went around to all the little groups and caught up on the gossip. The week went by as usual with the exception that the book she ordered was in. She went to pick up the Dream book from the library and started reading it right away. It was different than all of the other dream books. This one was more from the psychological point of view and not so much from the hocus pocus dream interpretation psychic point of view. She knew that dream interpretation is kind of hokey but she really just wanted to know why she dreamed like she did. She believed that dreams were the subconscious mind's way of trying to connect with the conscious mind. She never really studied psychology although she read some books on it in school. Basic brain waves and what part of the brain does what kind of stuff. She knew about Pavlov's dogs and the theory of Classical conditioning but she hadn't really thought about how that applied to anything but school.

She read a little here and there on her spare time and before she knew it, Friday was here. She went to work that day and thought about what she had read in the book. She read that we are resistant to ourselves and that is why our dreams are the way that they are. They are full of clues to the subconscious mind with mostly emotional attachments to them. She was guessing that our dreams are formed based on how we feel. She didn't know how accurate the book was but it was touching on something that made her think about it. She thought about the dreams that all contained the crazy killer with a knife that chased her. How would that relate to her life, to how she felt. She thought about the fear she felt that he was going to catch her and kill her. Then she asked herself, who chased her and made her feel afraid like that. Then it dawned on her. She was actually chased by that mean boy in the park. He had a knife and she was terrified as she ran from him because he said he was going to kill her. She watched him stab that man. That was the connection to the dream! It was the boy in the park. The crazy man chasing her with the knife was the boy in the park. Finally that dream had a connection to her real life. She didn't know how that was going to help her but she made the connection nonetheless. It was an answer.

She got off of work at one o'clock as usual. She went home, changed her clothes, washed her face and hands and brushed her hair. She made her usual pot of coffee and pulled out both of her to-go mugs. Before long, Joe was there to pick her up. He knocked lightly on her door. She felt confident today since she felt she made some headway with the connection. Hi Joe, come on in. She walked back to the kitchen and poured some coffee in her extra to-go mug and handed it to him. Here ya go, the cream and sugar are on the table, she said with a smile as she went to grab her purse.

They left in time as usual and went to the clinic. Raylynn checked in as usual and Joe found them a seat. As they sat there waiting for her appointment with Sara, they chatted a little about the meditation class and helping others. It wasn't much but Raylynn wanted to share that she helps where she can with the little things and with life being so difficult and unpredictable for her, it made it near impossible to make an ongoing commitment outside of her job. Reverend Joe assured her that the little things were enough and she can always consider volunteering for more as she becomes more available for it. Raylynn felt that she probably should do more but was satisfied, for now at least, doing what she felt she could.

Sara called her name; they walked back to her office and sat down at the little table. Sara opened the file and pulled out the time line. Let's see, where did we leave off, Sara said as she looked down at the time line. Oh yes, your 20th birthday. It was a good day, right? Sara said. Yep, my friends came and got me. They took me out for my birthday. We went to the corner pizza parlor and had a pizza party. I got so full on pizza I thought I was going to explode! Raylynn said as she giggled. I had such a good time that day. We made fun of each other and put on silly hats. My friend, Elizabeth, brought bubbles and she was blowing bubbles all over the place. Just a month or two after I got my second apartment, I was 20 years old and worked at CGN Grocers. It was the local grocery store not far from my apartment.

I didn't make enough to buy a car at the time so I rode a bike to work. The job paid for my apartment and Utilities and I had a few dollars left over for some food. I ate cheap and not very often. I got a roommate to share the expenses. Her name was Beth. She and I lived together for about 15 months. It was great until she met someone special and fell in love. She moved in with him which left me without a roommate. It was okay because I finally worked full time at the grocery store and could afford, barely, to live on my own. It was okay. I cut some corners such as going to the movies or out to eat with friends and things were good for a while.

What happened here? I was raped by a friend of the family. Vic was about my age but my parents liked him. They were helping him out and letting him stay at their place. He called me up one day and asked if he could come over for a few. I told him he could but I didn't have long I had to go grocery shopping but I had time for a visit. He came over and I invited him to come inside and he grabbed me and pushed me into my bedroom. He raped me although I screamed for him to stop and to get out; he just went on and did it. Sara interrupted for just a second to ask, "Did you tell anyone?" Yes, I told my mother and she told me I deserved it and that if I went to the police they wouldn't believe me. If I put out once in awhile these things wouldn't happen. I was devastated.

Sara looked down at the time line and seen the next event was an abortion. Tell me about this here Raylynn, what happened with this, Sara said as she pointed to the Abortion. Well, a month or two after the rape I found out I was pregnant. I was going to give it up for adoption but Vic told me he would do to it the same thing he did to me. I couldn't stand the thought and so I chose to have an abortion instead. I had a difficult time making that decision but I felt that I didn't have a choice. I couldn't go through the whole pregnancy to have him take the baby and rape it like he did me. I had the abortion and my mother called me a baby killer. Just to have the abortion I had to cross the picket line of the anti-abortion protesters. I told them they didn't know my situation but they didn't care then I had to deal with my mother calling me a baby killer. I left and didn't go back to my parents' house for about a year. I didn't want to deal with my mother any more. I couldn't deal with her petty lack of understanding or concern. Both of my parents took his side when I told them about the rape and neither of them was kind to me when I was faced with the decision I made to have the abortion.

Maybe if they were on my side and helped me get him locked up I might have made a different decision. I may have gone through with it and given the baby up for adoption. Who knows what could have happened. Sara said, you know Raylynn that the rape was not your fault. You didn't cause it to happen.

Raylynn thought about it for a minute and thought how much it felt like it was her fault and her mother made her feel like it was her fault. She nodded and fell silent for minute as tears streamed down her cheeks once again. I considered killing myself again after that happened. I just wanted to die. I just felt like the only reason I am alive is for men to hurt me, Raylynn said as she wiped away the tears. I was depressed for a long time after the rape and abortion. I got back together with Barry and we got married. Of course he started cheating on me almost immediately after we got married and he did throughout the whole time we were married. I left him and got a divorced a little more than four years later. He was so abusive. He would tell his friends how much he despised me and didn't want me then when his friends would make passes at me he would blame me.

I didn't like any of his friends, they were all low life kind of guys. I mean any guy who would make passes on their friend's wife regardless could not be all that good of a friend. He would beat me because of it. We would get into fights because he said I was leading them on. I would tell him I didn't and he would hit me and call me a liar. Maybe if he didn't tell them he wasn't interested in me they would have assumed he was and would have left me alone. I was so miserable. He was so hateful towards me. When he broke my arm I had enough. I left everything with Barry. I didn't even ask him for anything when I divorced him. I didn't want anything from him. He was such a jerk I figured just getting out was good enough and I moved on with my life. I just hated the life I had with that man.

Shortly after that I met up with Richard and we almost dated but that didn't work out at the time and then I got together briefly with Jerry Dansworth. He was a real winner. Sara interrupted, Well lets talk about him next time. I think we should end here and start with meditation before we go. Raylynn nodded. She felt so helpless when she thinks about what happened way back then. She didn't want to think about how mean they were to her. Did she deserve it in some way? Did she do something at some point in her life that made her deserve what they did to her? They completed their meditation and left the little office. She walked out to the waiting room where Reverend Joe was sitting. She said goodbye and walked over to Reverend Joe and together they walked out of the clinic.

As they walked to his car Reverend Joe noticed the distant expression on Raylynn's face. He helped her in the car and went around to the other side and got in. He looked over at Raylynn who was now buckling her seat-belt. You okay Ray? He asked with concern. Yep, she replied. How about a bite to eat at Jim's burgers? He said cheerfully. Sure, I could use a bite to eat she said as she looked at him and smiled. Okay Ray, I can see the distance in your eyes. I don't like it when you seem so far away. He said as grumpy as he was concerned. Why do you care so much what I am thinking or how I am doing? She sniped. Because I care about you Raylynn; I care about you more than you know, he said. Not knowing what he meant by that she just took a deep breath and said she was sorry for snapping at him.

They pulled into the parking lot of Jim's Burgers and Joe found a parking spot close to the door. Before they got out of the car Joe looked over at Raylynn and asked, what is bothering you Ray? Talk to me and tell me what's wrong, he pleaded. I was talking to Sara about my past relationships. It got so complicated sometimes and it was so bad at other times. You know Jerry Dansworth was so charming at first. He was nicer to me than any of the other men. He gave me flowers and other gifts and said nice things to me. Then we moved in together and one day he changed. I confided in him and told him about my parents and right before we broke up he beat me up and then told me horrible things like I enjoyed what my father did and that I liked to be abused. He went on for a week until he had me on the floor in the fetal position begging him to please just stop. He brought out a loaded gun and said it was ready when I was. He was trying to get me to kill myself. He was trying to get me to use a gun on myself to blow my brains out and end it all.

I don't know what he was thinking. What if I would have chosen to kill him instead? He was the one saying the mean things to me. What if I killed him then myself? I don't think I ever got together with anyone who was stable or kind even when I thought they were they always turned out to not be kind. Because of my past relationships I am afraid to get involved with anyone else. It seems as though I only attract jerks. I don't believe that Ray. I don't believe that you only attract jerks. I think you just have gotten involved with jerks in the past. Maybe your judgment has been impaired because of what your parents have done to you. Maybe you wanted to be loved and accepted so much but you believed you didn't deserve the good ones so you accepted any jerk who came along, he explained thoughtfully.

You are a good person Ray, and you deserve to be treated with kindness and respect and you have a right to be angry, he continued as if she had never heard those words before. She looked at him, shocked with his words. You say that to all the people you help, don't you? She asked. Ray, I believe what I am saying to you. I know you are a good person. I know you deserve to be loved and treated with kindness. You are a good person. When you realize that you will be able to accept love and kindness and you won't accept being treated any other way, he said firmly. She looked at him sitting there with one hand on his steering wheel and his other hand in his lap. She looked deep in his eyes and she knew he meant what he was saying. She couldn't help but feel like she was falling in love with him but she couldn't let herself feel that way for him. She knew he was right. When she could really feel like she deserved to be loved and treated kindly she would be ready to open up to the right man again. But for now, she didn't feel that. She just didn't know it for herself. She couldn't convince herself that she deserved to be loved kindly. She looked at him straight in the eye and sincerely said, thank you Joe.

He turned and put both hands on the steering wheel and said well, I hope you are hungry Ray, cuz I am starved. She smiled and said, yes Joe I am hungry, I can eat a whole burger to myself. She looked at him and smiled. He looked back at her with his puppy dog eyes and said, let's get inside and get our food ordered. After they walked in the door He asked her to find a seat. She went to the small room along the outside wall with all the windows and found a table with a great view of the parking lot. Before too long Joe was carrying a tray of food and two frozen colas. Raylynn loved the frozen colas at Jim's. It reminded her of the slushies she used to get when she was a kid only cola flavored instead of cherry. They ate and talked about her ex-husbands and boyfriends and others who wished her harm. He listened and told her she didn't deserve to be treated that way. It was them not her. She was glad that he listened. After they were finished he took her home and said good night.

Chapter 9

Promotion and a bonus

The weekend went by very quickly. Between work and church it went by quite well. She got to see Sandra and Joe's speech was brilliant as usual. He is very giving and kind and believes that everyone should do their part to make the world a better place. He gave another talk about helping others whenever we can. People are always more likely to help someone else if they are the recipient of help at one point. She thought about what he had said and was determined that she would try to be as helpful as she can when the opportunity would arise.

It was Monday afternoon and she was on her way out the door of the convenient store when Steve called her back in to talk to her. What is it Steve? She asked as she walked back in. She was a little concerned because Steve never does that unless it was serious. I was asked to give this to you when you finished your shift today. I almost forgot, He huffed. He seemed completely out of breath as he stood there huffing and puffing while holding an envelope in his hand. Here Ray, Open it. She took the envelope out of his hand and opened it. Inside of it was a check for $100 made out to her. Wow, what is this for? She asked. She was puzzled as to why she would have been given this. She thought for a moment that maybe she was being fired.

It is a bonus Ray, We all got one. We did so well over the last month that we got a bonus. They were happy with our performance. Ben at the main office said that they have started a new rewards program. if we hit our mark in sales and in other areas we will get a bonus at the end of the month. He said excitedly. Ray, I also wanted to talk to you about something else. What is it Steve? She asked. Debbie put in her notice, she is leaving us and I am going to need a new assistant manager. I want to put in for you to be my new assistant manager but I want to ask you if you want the job before I do. It means you will be on call, training new hires and I will work it so you can keep your current time shift but you will have to work more hours. What do you say Ray? Do you want the job?

Raylynn couldn't believe what she was hearing. She was being put up for a promotion. She has been with this store for about three years now and never expected to ever get a promotion. Could she handle the hours? How many more hours a week will it be and I have an appointment every Friday that I just can't miss. Well, I will be going to nights and you will have to open in the mornings. That means you will have to be here by 6am and you won't get off work until 6pm and you can have Friday and Sunday off. I will work out the details. I still have to get it approved so no promises, he said to her as confidently as he could. I would love to have the position, she squealed. Good, then I will go ahead and put in the request. Oh and by the way it is a $2.00 per hour pay raise too, he said with a smile. That's awesome, more hours and pay. That would do just great, she said. Okay Ray, see you tomorrow. As soon as I hear back I will let you know. Okay Steve, thanks, she said as she walked out the door. As she got in her car she thought about the pay raise. Not only am I going to get a pay raise but I will be getting a few more hours. I will be able to get a couple new dresses and some dress clothes. I will be able to look nice when I want to, she thought.

She went home and walked up to her apartment. Barbara was coming down the stairs just as she unlocked her door. Hi, Ray, she said as she reached the bottom stair. Hi Barbara, Raylynn said cheerfully. You are getting in from work a few minutes late tonight, is everything okay? She asked. Am I that predictable? Raylynn asked as she opened her door. Actually Ray, you are the most reliable person with the most reliable schedule. So what's kept you? Barbara said. Well, my boss wanted to talk to me for a minute is all. She said. Nothing bad I hope, she said trying to pry for information. No, nothing bad, they are starting a new reward program for employees and he wanted to tell me about it is all. Raylynn was careful not to give too much information. Barbara is one of the types that you only give her information that is okay for everyone to know.

Raylynn stood there listening to Barbara talk about the couple across the way and the family in the corner apartment. She finally seen a break in the conversation and said she had to get inside and get some housework done before she goes to bed. Barbara was understanding at that and said she had to get going anyway. She announced that she was going out to dinner with her friends. Have a good time, Raylynn said with a smile and slipped inside her apartment.

She put her things down on the sofa and took her phone out of her pocket. She immediately called Sandra who was on her way to the food kitchen. She told Sandra all about what Steve had said about the promotion and bonus. She was so happy about the good news that she called everyone she knew who might answer their phone. She was excited to be considered for a promotion and she could use the money. She wasn't sure if she could handle the hours but she knew it would probably keep her mind off of things.

She made fried chicken for dinner. She made green beans because she was very careful not to eat foods like potatoes or corn because of the starch in it. She was getting older and didn't want to weigh herself down with extra pounds even if it were only a few. She had to stay as fit as she could so that she could fight off any attackers who might want to hurt her. She often had the feeling that she could be attacked at any given time and had to be able to protect herself. She knew she was just being hyper vigilant but she couldn't help it. She had to feel safe and being thin made her feel safe.

It was close to bedtime so she went into her room and put on her pajamas. I wonder how long it will be before I find out if I got the promotion or not? She thought as she brushed her teeth. She washed her face and hands then went to lay down in bed. She thought about becoming the assistant manager and what it will be like as she waited for sleep to overcome her. That night she went to sleep and had a dream that she was being attacked. Some crazy man was attacking her and she fought back. She dreamed that she got the best of him. The next thing she knew she was kicking him in the stomach. She was beating the crap out of him. She was so angry she was yelling at him and just kicking him.

She suddenly woke up. Her blanket was thrashed about and she was sweating. She must have been kicking in her sleep while she dreamed. She was a little concerned about her violent dreams. She has never thought violent things before and she was always careful not to harm anyone. She never dreamed like that before. She felt justified and guilty at the same time. Justified because he was going to hurt her and she protected herself but guilty because she did it because she was so freaking angry and all she wanted to do was hurt him. She just wanted to beat the living daylights out of him and let him know how it feels.

She looked at the clock and it was 4am. She still had two and a half hours left before she had to get up and get ready for work. She lay back down and closed her eyes. She was still so tired she knew she could go back to sleep. She turned over and went back to sleep quickly. It seemed like she just fell asleep when her alarm went off. It was 6:30am and she couldn't believe it was time to get up already. Raylynn got up and went to the kitchen to start her pot of coffee then headed to bathroom to take her shower. She thought of her 4am dream and wondered why she is having dreams like that. She is not usually a violent person yet she dreamed she kicked someone. She felt so angry when she woke up. She just couldn't believe that she would feel that way.

As she toweled off after her shower she thought about the day and wondered if Steve would get back with her by the end of the week about the promotion. She put on her uniform and got her coffee and breakfast then went to work. When she arrived promptly 10 minutes early as usual she walked straight to the back and got ready for her shift. As she moved to the front of the store she said good morning to Steve. Good morning Ray, he replied. Just so you know I put in the request and it is only a matter of days before I hear back, he said excitedly. That's great, Raylynn said with a smile. I'm patient but I was wondering if I am going to get training before Debbie leaves, she asked. Um, I am hoping that Debbie can start your training then I will continue after she leaves. She should go over the main part of the job before you start but you already know how to do most of it, he said. She looked at him for a second and realized that the assistant manager only had a few extra details to handle while the rest of the job is what she already does.

She finished her shift at the store and went home. When she checked her voice-mail she heard the message from the library. They had the dream book she wanted. She looked at the clock and realized she had time to go pick it up so that is just what she did. She got to the library and picked up the book. She went home, made dinner and read for awhile. Later that evening she got ready for bed. She sat on the sofa with a hot cup of cocoa and just thought about what she had read. She thought about her dreams and how her dreams are the connection to her subconscious. If she can figure out her dreams she might be able to understand what it is that makes her have some of her nightmares. She put her empty cup in the sink and went to bed.

The night started off with out any problems but by 2am she was awakened by one of the crazy killer dreams. The killer was chasing her and reverend Joe. He threatened both of them. She crawled in bed with Reverend Joe and tried to wake him. Help she cried. Wake up Joe and help. It was a bunk bed and the crazy killer came to the side of the bed and Joe was by the wall. Joe started to stir and the crazy killer said if he wakes up I am going to kill him. She was terrified then the dream switched to her and Joe running from the killer. He was coming for them and was going to kill them when he catches them. They ran into this bathroom and Raylynn turned off the light to keep the killer from seeing them. If it is dark the killer can't see them. Next thing she knew the light was on and they were standing there next to the killer. The killer turned the light on and she quickly turned it off. The killer turned the light back on and raised his knife standing over her ready to stab her. She suddenly woke up gasping for breath. She had beads of sweat on her face. She got up and went to get a cup of water and sit on the sofa as she always did after awaking from a nightmare.

She sat on the sofa and thought about her dream. What does it mean? Why do I always dream that I am running from a crazy killer? She thought about the book and asked herself, who is the crazy killer? Who does he represent? She thought about the bed and the bathroom and realized the killer in the bed and the bathroom was a representation of her father. Her father abused her in her bed and the bathroom and her nightmare has something to do with that. But why the chasing and the knife. Who chased me with a knife? She thought. She thought for a minute and realized that the boy in the park chased her around the trees at the back of the park where he stabbed that man. She realized the crazy killer was the boy in the park, her father, and her rapists. It was all of them. The crazy killer represented all of her abusers, attackers and rapists. She sat there on the sofa and sobbed. She realized the part that each of them play in her dreams. Her nightmares were tied to reality. She found her connection.

She went back to bed and just laid there thinking about all that had happened to her. It seemed to be hours before she fell back to sleep. She woke up to her alarm bright and early. She got up and Went to the store. Steve noticed she wasn't well rested. What's wrong Ray? Are you getting sick again, he asked. Nope, just had a hard time sleeping last night is all, she replied. The day dragged on for what seemed like forever. The day always goes by slowly when she is tired. 4pm finally rolled around and she was free to leave. She was going to meet with Joe tonight and she wanted to tell him about her realization she had last night. She got home and changed her clothes, washed her face and hands as usual and made a half a pot of coffee and sat there for a minute. She just thought about the men in her life and how there seemed to be very few good ones in it.

She thought about how angry she has been and realized she had a reason to be angry. She started feeling even more angry as she thought about it. It was time to leave and she finished her coffee. She got to the Dark Roast a few minutes early but Reverend Joe was already there. He met her at the door to Coffee house. Hey Ray, another tough night? He asked. Yep she said. But I had a realization I want to talk to you about so when we get our order I will fill you in, she said with a smile. She was very tired but she was excited about what she discovered about herself. They went inside and she picked the table by the window. She sat there and watched out the window while Reverend Joe got their order.

Within minutes he arrived with two cups of coffee and a pocket full of cream and sugar. The sandwiches should be ready soon, he said as he sat down. So what is this realization you were talking about? He asked with curiosity. Raylynn started to tell him about her dream discovery and who the crazy killer is in her dream. She told him about the book she picked up and how it helped her make that discovery. She told him about how angry she has been and about her dream of her kicking the attacker. He listened quietly with a serious expression on his face. He didn't make fun of her or minimize any of her experiences or her discovery. She finished then asked, what do you think Joe? I think you have a right to be angry. I don't know how the discovery will help you except maybe to understand yourself a little more. Maybe you needed to know that to understand your anger. You know you have a good reason to be angry and it is normal to want to hurt your attackers. Get angry Ray. You should be angry. He reached out and squeezed her hand. Don't feel guilty for feeling angry Ray. You should be angry; you have a right to be angry.

The girl behind the counter called out, JOE! Your order is ready! Joe looked at Ray and winked and said, I'll be right back with our food. He got up and headed toward the counter. Raylynn watched him with affection. She was really beginning to have feelings for him but she didn't want to say anything. He was always so nice to her and he really is very good looking. She wasn't sure if what she was feeling was real or if it is just a repeat of the past. Is she really falling for this guy or is it just that he is nice to her. She wasn't so sure and before she accepts it she has to be sure. She watched him get the tray with the sandwiches laying on it. As he carried it to their table she thought about him and wondered what life would be like if she never had any of her issues. Would she be questioning her feelings right now if she had never been abused? I will never know the answer to that question and some day that question won't matter, she thought as Joe placed the tray on the table.

She smiled at him as she picked up her sandwich. She began to unwrap her sandwich. It looked delicious as usual and she was so hungry she could hear her stomach growl. So, whatchya got planned for tonight's lesson? She asked then took a bite of her sandwich. I have a video planned for the group tonight he said with pride. A video? She asked what kind of video? Oh, a movie called Pay it Forward. I thought it would be a good movie to watch tonight and I was wondering if you would sit with me while it played, he said quietly. Um, sure Joe, I would love to sit with you and Sandra both, she said. It will be fun. So why the movie? Didn't you have anything planned to talk about? Oh yes, it will go with the Sunday's sermon. It is a really good movie Ray, when you see it I think you will understand why I chose it, he said then took another bite of his sandwich.

Raylynn told him about her dreams and how angry she has been feeling whenever she thinks about what "they" did to her. He listened quietly as he always did. When she had finished telling him about it he just sat there and said you should be angry Ray. What they did to you was horrible and they deserve to be punished. No one should have to go through what you went through and you have every right to be angry. She listened intently although she still didn't feel comfortable feeling all that anger festering inside her. Don't worry Ray, someday you will not feel so angry. Someday you will get past it and you won't feel this way.

Before long it was time to leave. Reverend Joe reached out and squeezed her hand like he always does and said, you are going to be okay, What you are feeling is normal. You always know what to say Joe. You always make me feel better. Thank you, she said with a sheepish grin. He patted her hand and said we better get going Ray; I have to get this television and

DVD player set up for tonight. It's going to take me a few minutes extra. Okay Joe, she replied. I have to stop at the GoMart and get some gas I will meet you there, she said with certainty. Okay Ray. See you there then he walked away. She got up and walked to her car. She got in and turned the key. Like an old faithful dog the car started right up. She thought of all of the things she had that was a blessing. She had a job and a car. She was happy with her apartment and she might get a promotion. Things were looking good for her right now and she said a short prayer thanking the universe for looking out for her.

She knew it could be worse; in fact it has been worse. She stopped to get gas then went to the church. When she arrived she seen that Joe had already got the television and DVD player set up and ready to go. People were already starting to arrive. Sandra showed up and pulled her around the room collecting gossip. They were all excited about what they were going to see. All they knew is that there was going to be a movie tonight. Raylynn didn't let on that she knew what it was. She told Sandra they were going to sit with Reverend Joe. Sandra teased a little then let it go.

Reverend Joe saved them a seat up front near the set to make it easier in case of any technical difficulties. He called everyone's attention to get them in their seats and quieted down. He got up and talked for a minute about giving help to others when someone helps you. He suggested passing on the kindness. Raylynn rolled her eyes because she knew what this was about. More of his "help others" and "be kind to others", not that she had a problem with it but it seemed to be the main motto. She felt bad because she didn't feel she had anything to offer others and every time someone brought up helping others she felt a little frustrated, like her hands were tied and she couldn't do anything.

She watched the movie and loved it. Reverend Joe was right; she understood where he was going with it. She may not be able to help anyone right now but eventually she will be able to help others. She will be okay someday and when that day happens she will be able to pay it forward. After the movie was over it was already 9:30ish and she needed to get home because she had to get up early tomorrow. She said good night to Sandra and waved good-bye to Reverend Joe and slipped out and went home.

Thursday morning she got up as usual but she had this feeling like today was going to be a really good day. When she arrived at work Steve pulled her aside and told her she will begin training on Monday and she would see a difference in her paychecks once she has gone through two full weeks of training. She was so excited that she didn't think her day could get any better. She had a great day and was elated that she was finally chosen to become the assistant manager. Steve liked her because she was usually early, dependable and she rarely made a mistake not to mention she was particular at how she did her job even on her bad days.

She went home and opened a bottle of cheap wine and poured herself a small glass in celebration then called Sandra and told her the good news. Sandra was happy for her as usual. That was the best part about

Sandra. She has always been truly happy for Raylynn when something good happened for her. Raylynn went into her room and put on her pajamas and laid on the bed thinking about what it was going to be like. Then she realized she wouldn't be able to make it to meet with Joe on Wednesdays any more. She was a little upset about that but the extra pay made it worth it. She needed the money and maybe they can make up the time somewhere else. She left a message for Joe knowing he wouldn't be home until after 10pm. She told him about her promotion and that she is not going to be able to meet on Wednesdays. She said she didn't know what her schedule was going to be like exactly yet but when she finds out maybe they can make arrangements to meet on another day of the week.

She climbed into bed and went to sleep. She had some disturbing dreams that Richard and his friends came into her workplace and were harassing her. She dreamed she had a baseball bat and she had to defend herself. She dreamed she beat them with the bat. Her dreams were all relatively the same. An abuser comes in and she beats the daylights out of them. She got up Friday morning not knowing what to think of her dreams. She didn't consider herself a violent person and didn't quite understand why she was being so violent in her dreams. She went off to work and had a great day. She got off at 1pm as usual and went home and managed her normal routine. She made a pot of coffee and sat there and just relaxed for a while as she drank a couple of cups. Joe arrived a few minutes earlier than usual.

Congratulations on your promotion Ray he said as she invited him inside. Thanks Joe, she said with a big smile. Do you want to use the to-go mug for a cup of coffee? She asked as she walked toward the cupboard. Sure thing Ray, Joe said as he moved toward her. She handed him the to-go mug and he poured himself a cup of coffee then headed to the dining table to add his cream and sugar. I am going to miss our Wednesday visits but it is worth it since you got a promotion and all, he said. Will you still be able to make it to Wednesday night service? He asked in a low tone slightly frowning. I am not sure, she said curling her lip. I will find out what my hours are going to be on Monday I think, or at least that is when the training starts. What about counseling? He asked with concern. Steve said my Friday should stay the same but I will have to work a full day on Saturdays and more hours the rest of the week. They sat down and chatted about work for a few minutes then they were off to see Sara.

She checked in while he got them a seat close to the door where Sara will call her name. She walked over and sat down. She looked at Joe who was sitting there with his head bowed and hands folded. He looked as though he was having a few words with his deity and she didn't want to disturb him. It was not very long before Sara stepped out and called her name. Raylynn got up and met Sara at the door. They walked through the hallway with small chit chat until they came to the door of her office. Sara opened the door and Raylynn walked in and sat down in her usual spot. Sara sat down and opened the file. They were still working on the time line. How have you been doing this week, Sara asked. Good except I have been dealing with a bit of anger, Raylynn replied. Who are you angry with? Sara asked. Raylynn responded by explaining everything including the violent dreams.

Anger is a good thing Raylynn, as long as you are dealing with it in a healthy way. Tell me how you are dealing with it. Sara said. Raylynn explained how she puts it away and shoves it deep down inside so she doesn't have to deal with it. She was always taught that anger was a bad thing and that she should never allow herself to be angry. Sara explained to her how anger is a necessary part of healing and that she should always allow herself to feel angry but the important part is expressing anger in a healthy way. Raylynn thought about it and decided to give it a try; the next time she felt angry she will scream in a pillow or punch the bed when she wakes up from one of those dreams to see how it makes her feel. She remembered her promotion at that moment and blurted it out. I got a promotion at work. The promotion was a big deal for Raylynn because she usually got promotions pretty quickly and this was the first time it took 3 years to get one. Sara smiled and said, that is great. Will you need to change your appointment times? Sara asked. No, I don't think so Raylynn replied. That is really great news, how do you feel about it? Sara asked. It has its pro's and con's, she replied.

Do you feel you can comply with the added duties, Sara asked. Yes, I believe I can and I can use the money too. It means more per hour and more hours which will give me enough hours to buy some new clothes in a month or so, Raylynn said. Good, good. There was a brief moment of silence then Sara said lets see; where were we on your time line? Raylynn was sick of going over the time line. She hated talking about all that stuff, especially the bad stuff. She looked down at the time line and pointed at the event "Maria Died". Tell me about what happened here, she said plainly.

Maria was my only friend at the time. She was always there for me. She would bring delicious food over and sit and visit for awhile. She was from Guatemala and she didn't have many friends here. She would talk about how badly Americans treated her because she didn't speak good English. Maria was a wonderful person and a great cook. I gained 10 pounds the year I knew her. She was the only person who didn't seem to want to use me that year. I loved having her around. She was an older woman in her 40's and she had high cholesterol and was a little over weight. She always wanted me to walk with her but I was always too tired, emotionally and physically. One day I seen an ambulance at her house, I later asked her husband what had happened and he said she had a stroke. She didn't make it. She died a little while later in the hospital. I was heartbroken. I couldn't believe I lost my only friend. She was the only one who would sit and just chat with me. My boss came to me shortly after and asked me what was going on with me because my work performance was suffering.

Tears rolled down Raylynn's cheeks as she talked about her friend. Sara listened quietly as Raylynn spoke. Raylynn sat and cried a moment and when she was ready to move on Sara guided her to the next event. You met Jerry Dansworth, and it was a good thing, Sara stated. Raylynn replied yes, he was so nice to me for the first year we were together. We did all kinds of things together and he taught me how to cook outdoors. It was wonderful for the first year. By the end of the first year I was madly in love with him but then he started treating me badly. Within a year and a half our relationship turned full swing. The next thing I know he is cheating and calling me names and telling me I liked all of the abuse in my life. One final day he kept stabbing at me with his words. He had me so hurt by using what I had confided in him about the abuse I had endured to hurt me even more. I was in the fetal position on the kitchen floor crying and begging him to stop. He went into the bedroom and pulled out a loaded gun and said to me, "it is ready when you are" then he laid the gun on the counter and walked back to the bedroom. He was trying to destroy me by attempting to make me suicidal.

He was hoping that he could hurt me so badly that I would kill myself that day. After he walked back to the room I realized why he was saying all of those horrible things to me that hurt so badly coming from him a man whom I loved dearly. I stood up, picked up the receiver of my landline phone and called a friend and told her what had happened. She came and got me and I went with her and she parked under a shade tree and I told her what he did and that I had to leave him. She invited me to stay with her until I could find a place and so we drove back and I grabbed some of my belongings and went to her place. I found a place of my own two weeks later and went to get the rest of my things.

I cried every day for the next 6 months of my life. I was so heartbroken and depressed I cried every second I was alone. I cried myself to sleep every night and I cried until my body ached on my days off of work. I couldn't believe that anyone could be so cruel. What he did was worse than any beating I had ever had. He nearly destroyed me with his words but it was so unfounded that it didn't make sense. What he was doing didn't make sense until he pulled out his gun and I knew. It became obvious at that point. I don't know why he didn't just break up with me. I don't understand why he hated me so much he felt he had to destroy me to make me leave.

Just breaking up would have been enough to hurt me. We could have sat down and talked about it rationally like adults. But he chose to do it that way. I don't know why he wanted me dead so badly. His plan could have gone horribly wrong had I went the other way and killed him first. It takes someone completely unstable to kill themselves and unstable means unpredictable. I could have killed him. Sometimes I wish I would have shot him. I wish I would have at least taken the gun and put it to his head and scared the crap out of him but I didn't do any of those things. I let him off easy by leaving him instead. I don't know how people can be so mean and nasty like what he did.

How are you feeling right now Raylynn? Sara asked. I feel Angry I want to hurt him. I want to hurt him and everyone who has abused me in my life! She shouted. I hate that guy. He isn't even a man. He is a low life weasel dirty rotten bag of scum. I want something horrible to happen to him. I want him to be destroyed the way he tried to destroy me. I hate him! It's normal to feel angry Ray. I want to get even Ray said with tears streaming down her face. How about if we try to meditate now before you leave today? Raylynn wiped away the stream from her tear streaked face and said okay. They did a meditation and Raylynn was brought back to her calm center once again.

They walked out of the small office and went back out to the waiting room. Raylynn felt better this time. She felt stronger than she has on previous visits. She walked up to Reverend Joe and smiled at him and said let's get out of her. They walked out and got in the car. Joe looked at her and said you know Ray; you are going to be alright. Raylynn looked at him and simply said, I know.

Chapter 10

The New Job

Friday night was surprisingly calm for Raylynn. She didn't have any nightmares or dreams about hurting people. She felt well rested Saturday when she got up and got ready for work in no time. Today she knew she would be stocking shelves like she always does on Saturdays. She got to work and Steve was already there as usual but there was one of the other employees there also. Usually it was just her and Steve on Saturdays. She clocked in and then walked up to Steve and asked why Roger was there stocking shelves. Steve said well Ray, I wanted to get a head start on your management training and so I needed someone else to stock the shelves. Are you ready to learn some new stuff? He asked with a grin. Sure, she said although she wasn't sure at all.

She worked a full day and didn't leave until 5pm. Steve taught her how to price merchandise and what to do with the time cards. He taught her about the machines and when they should be cleaned. He talked about the schedule and how it is run and how it will be rearranged for the next two weeks. He briefly went over how to accept shipments and do inventory. By the time she went home that night, her mind was swirling with new information to absorb. She didn't realize how much she would have to do now that she was the assistant manager. They talked about her new schedule and what it was going to be. She was going to be working from 7am to 5pm every day except Friday and Sunday. Friday she will keep her half day and Sunday she will have off. Steve was going to be taking Debbie's shift and she is going to be taking his with a slight difference. She will have to work Sunday during the day if Tom or Nicolette call in sick and he will work all the night shifts.

She thought about all of the hours she could be working and how much money she would be making. She was so happy about that and with counseling going much better now she knew she was going to be all right. When she got home she made herself a hot cup of Chamomile tea with a little honey to help her relax, took her shoes off and sat on the sofa and thought about all the details of the job she had learned over the course of the day. She was beat but over all she had a great day.

She slept well that night and woke up Sunday morning bright and early at 7:33 am. She didn't even feel tired and worn out like she usually did. She got up and made her coffee and took her shower. She started giving her apartment an overhaul cleaning. It is November and thanksgiving was going to come around soon. She doesn't go to her parents for holidays any more and she was wondering what she should do for thanksgiving. She could make a little game hen and traditional side dishes for herself.

Treat herself to a good meal. She was really on a cleaning spree when she heard her phone ring. She walked over and looked to see who was calling. It was

Sandra. Hi Sandra, she said cheerfully. Hi Ray, are you busy, can you talk a minute? Sandra blurted. Well, I'm doing some cleaning but I have a minute to talk, why, what's up? She replied. Well, my parents are having a big thanksgiving meal this year and I was wondering if you would come so I would have someone my own age to talk to. The whole family is going to be here and I need someone on my side, she giggled. Well, I have no plans and there is no one I would rather get into trouble with than you Sandra, Raylynn replied with a big smile. Awesome, I will let my parents know you are coming. See you tonight. Then she said goodbye.

Raylynn hung up the phone and resumed cleaning. Before she knew it the clock already struck one and it was time to get ready to meet with Joe. She hurried in to get ready and realized she was a mess and got a second shower. She giggled to herself at the thought that she should have waited until after cleaning to take her shower this morning, what a mess I am. She got ready and rushed out the door to meet with Joe. She got there just in time to pull in right beside him. He parked right in front for a change and she got the spot right next to him. What luck she thought. My luck is changing and things are getting better she thought as she got out of the car. Reverend Joe was by her side in no time and they walked into the Dark Roast together.

She was so excited about yesterday she couldn't wait to tell him all about it. She talked to him about all the cool things she learned about her new job yesterday. She chattered in line all the way up to the counter. Joe chuckled and said, I'm glad for you Ray. I am glad you are enjoying your job. It's really good to see you get excited about something. Oh, and I am too, she replied. It has been a long time since I have felt this way. I feel like I have accomplished something when I really didn't do much at all, with that she giggled. He motioned toward the empty tables by the window and said, "Go ahead and get us a seat, Ray". She happily said okay then walked over to pick their table. Their usual table was taken so she sat at the table next to it. There was still a good view out the window but she didn't stare out the window this time. This time she watched Joe pick up the coffee, walk over to the condiment bar and stuff his shirt pocket full of cream and sugar. She felt happy like life was finally giving her a shot at happiness even if only for the day.

He walked to their table and sat the coffee down pulled out the cream and sugar and piled it in the middle of the table. Raylynn sat there and just grinned. What? He shrieked with a chuckle. Why are you staring at me with that weird grin on your face? He asked with a smile. I'm really happy Joe. I am going to go shopping with the first check after my promotion is final. I am going to buy myself some new clothes. I could use some jeans and a couple of dresses. My clothes are looking really sad and it's time I treated myself, she said. Well don't get too far ahead of yourself now, he said. You should save some money back for a while and wait for a sale so you can get the most for your money, he said then took a sip of his hot coffee. She thought for a moment and agreed that would be a great idea.

They sat and talked awhile then went their separate ways. She had to go home and change and finish some of her light duty cleaning before church and he had to prepare for the service. She went home and finished her cleaning then got ready for church. She headed out to church when Barbara stopped her to ask how she was doing. I'm great Raylynn said. I got a promotion which means a little more money to get what I need around the house. Wow, that's good news Ray, I hope you enjoy the new job, Barbara said with a smile. Are you still seeing that man that picks you up on Fridays? She asked. He is just a friend Barbara, she said as they walked in the direction of her car. They arrived at her car and Raylynn said, I've got to get going, I don't want to be late to church. Oh sure thing Ray, go ahead get going, I will see you later, Barbara said with a friendly pat on Raylynn's back.

Raylynn got in her car and headed to church. When she arrived she found Sandra talking to Gerty. Sandra excused herself and ran over to Raylynn and said you will never guess what the latest gossip is Ray. Oh I can imagine, she said. Those two old women already have you and Reverend Joe Getting married in the spring, ha ha ha, she laughed. Oh please, Joe and I are just friends. Joe eh. You two are a little informal so I guess you won't mind that Reverend Joe is coming to my house for thanksgiving.

You invited Reverend Joe to your house with your parents on thanksgiving? Raylynn Shrieked. Is he going to be your date? She asked. Raylynn was beginning to feel betrayed by Sandra. No, no, silly, I don't want to date Reverend Joe. I invited him because he doesn't have anyone to spend thanksgiving with. He would be alone. I figured the three of us could hang out and it would give you someone you know besides me. Are you upset that he is coming Ray? She asked. Um, no, I guess not. I'm sorry Sandra I don't know why I was so upset. It's cool Ray, come on and let's see what is up with the Harveys. Sandra pulled Ray around the room as usual.

After the services Raylynn had a great idea to go out for ice cream. Hey Sandra do you wanna go get ice cream? My treat, she said with a silly grin on her face. You mean right now? She asked. Yep! Right now, lets go to the Lions Den and get an Ice cream sundae, Raylynn chirped. Okay sure, sounds deelish, Sandra said as she put on her coat. Let's get the heck outta here and get us some ice cream, she said as she pushed her nose in the air.

They went out for ice cream. Raylynn told her all about her new job position at the store and how Saturday he started training her early. She was not going to be stocking shelves or cleaning bathrooms any more. They had a good visit and Raylynn enjoyed her ice cream. She had a banana split with pineapple and cherry topping and smothered with chocolate syrup. She hardly ever ate treats like ice cream these days. She had to stay slim so she could run if she needed to. She went home happy and a little bloated from the ice cream. Well, she said out loud, soon I will be an assistant manager. She said it out loud again. Assistant Manager. She went into the bathroom and looked in the mirror and said, Hi, I am Raylynn the Assistant Manager. She chuckled at the sound of it. She got ready for bed and made herself a cup of chamomile tea with honey. Chamomile was her favorite tea and it always made her feel more relaxed.

She thought about the anxiety and realized she hadn't had an anxiety attack in almost 3 days. Her dreams were changing and so was her anxiety. She wondered what it all meant. Was she getting closer to being a whole genuine person? Was she really on her way to being normal or at least close to it? She didn't know the answer to those questions but she wanted to know. She realized she was going through changes. She was changing and becoming stronger. I wonder how long it will take to heal from all of this sadness and anger she thought.

She went into her room and went to bed. She didn't have any bad dreams about the abuse or rapes but she had a bad dream about work. She dreamed that there was a problem with the register and everyone was coming up short at the end of their shifts. She tried to call the representative about it but couldn't find the number then they got some new merchandise like kids T-shirts and bookmarks. They had to promote the new items as people checked out. She woke up feeling stressed out. She knew it was because of the new job position. She was feeling a bit insecure about it and it was coming out in her dreams.

She got up and got ready for work. She thought about the new training she was going to have today with Debbie. She always liked Debbie and thought she would be there forever. She felt silly about her dream and told herself that she would be able to do this job easily. I have been on this job for 3 years now and I know everything there is to know about being a cashier and I should be able to manage the job just fine, she told herself. She went off to work and arrived a few minutes early. She clocked in and got a cup of coffee then walked up to the counter where Debbie was standing. Steve isn't going to be here? Raylynn asked. She was a little confused. Steve is taking my shift and I am taking this one so I can train you. Steve said he went over a few things with you on Saturday so this should be easy. They went over some more of the job duties and discussed how to handle complaints and disagreements. There was no third person there today just the two of them so training went a little slow as they went about the daily transactions and gasoline sales.

She couldn't leave until 5pm when her new shift was about to end. Debbie said well, you might as well get used to the new shift detail. Meet me here at 7am so I can show you what you need to do when you first get here in the morning. Raylynn nodded. Steve was coming on the job as Raylynn was leaving. Hey Ray, how's the training going? Steve asked cheerfully. It's going good, she replied. I will be here at 7 tomorrow morning. That is the earliest I have ever been to work ever in my life. I will see how it goes tomorrow, she said with a giggle. Steve said, awe Ray, you will get used to it. I woke up this morning at 5 as usual and had a hard time falling back to sleep myself. It will be okay.

You will see. Well, good night you two, See you in the morning Debbie, she said as she walked out the door.

She went home and made some fried chicken and green beans for dinner then relaxed for the rest of the evening. She felt a little lonely for the first time in a long time. She actually wanted some company tonight. I wonder what everyone is up to she thought as she picked up her phone. She couldn't help but feel a little anxiety as she scrolled through her list of numbers. Then she realized that the person she wanted to visit with was Reverend Joe and He was at the shelter tonight. Maybe we can plan something together tomorrow night she thought. She sent him a text that read, "I have to work late from now on and I was wondering if you wanted to change our Wednesday meeting to Tuesday night?" She wasn't sure what he would say. A few minutes later she got a text back. It read, "Sure, you want to start tomorrow at 7pm?" She was happy with that and texted back to him, "its perfect see you tomorrow".

She felt happy that he messaged her back and didn't have a problem meeting on Tuesdays. She got up and went to the kitchen and made some Chamomile tea then went to her room and put on her Pajamas. She sat on the sofa while she drank her tea and prepared for sleep. She crawled into bed at 9:30pm and hoped she could fall asleep quickly. She laid there for a few minutes then drifted off to sleep. It was an uneventful night except for the dream that her mother was out in an orchard picking apples and brought in this creepy crawly thing and put in her hair. She was terrified to move. Raylynn finally got the nerve to smack the creepy thing out of her hair and Raylynn just yelled at her mother for being so mean. She wanted to smack her for doing it. Raylynn woke up and realized it was just a stupid dream. She quickly fell back to sleep for a change. She got up in the morning at 5:30 and got ready for work. She was dragging a bit and decided she would go to bed earlier every night she could and would sleep in extra long on her day off.

She went to work and got there about 10 minutes to 7 and waited for Debbie to arrive. Debbie arrived at 3 minutes to 7 and rushed to the door. Raylynn met her at the door cheerfully. Debbie showed her what she needed to do and went about the training as usual. Raylynn was beat when she got off work but Steve was cheery as always when he arrived as she was leaving. Bye Debbie, Bye Steve she called out as she walked out the door. She went home and washed her face and hands then changed her clothes. She was going to meet with Joe tonight at 7 and wanted to hurry up and eat something and have a strong cup of coffee before she left to meet with him.

She arrived at The Dark Roast about 7:03 and Joe was already there waiting for her. She walked inside and over to his table and sat down. You look a bit tired Ray, Joe said. I am, she said leaning her chin in her hand. I am exhausted. I got to work before 7am and I am extremely tired she said drearily. Hmmm, maybe Tuesday nights aren't such a good thing. Do you want a cup of coffee? He asked. Yep a cup of coffee would be good. Joe went up to the counter and ordered a cup of regular coffee and came back with two muffins along with her cup of coffee. I wasn't sure if you had eaten so I grabbed a muffin for you, he said as he sat the muffin down in front of her. She smiled and thanked him for being so thoughtful. You deserve a break Ray. You will get used to your new hours soon enough. How are you doing otherwise? He asked as he looked at her with his puppy dog eyes.

I am doing good Joe. For the first time in years I actually felt lonely last night. I actually wanted company. I never feel lonely. I usually feel safe when I'm alone in my home. I mean considering whenever there is someone there I usually end up getting hurt in some way, ya know? Well, maybe you are getting to a different part of your life and you are about ready to invite someone into it. Yeah maybe, she said. You know Ray, when bad things happen to us; we have a choice to heal or to hang on to the pain. You have made the decision to heal and it really depends on you, on how far you go with it. Sara can't heal you; a Psychiatrist can't heal you only you can decide how much you heal.

There comes a time when you must decide to let go of the pain if you are to go further. Let go of what has hurt you. Only you can make that decision and only you can let go. You will know when it is time to let go of the pain that keeps you in a mental prison of emotional agony. The dreams, the anxiety, the depression, all of it. Maybe you are on your next step in healing. He said as non-judgmental as he possibly could manage. You are a strong woman Ray, you may not feel like you are but you have the strength to pull yourself out of the funk. Someday you will see what I mean. Ray sat there in silence as she let his words sink in.

You're right, I know you are right I just wish I could feel that you're right, she sighed. It's getting late, I need to get going. I need to get home and get some rest, she said as she stood up. He said, I don't want you to think I was lecturing you Ray, I just see such high potential in you and I know you hold the key to the door. Unlock it and let yourself loose on the world. You can do amazing things, I know you can. They walked out of the Dark Roast together as Reverend Joe gave her that pep talk. Thank you Joe. I appreciate what you are saying. I really do, she said. She opened her car door and said good night.

She got into the little Fiero and drove home. She wearily went into her little apartment and got ready for bed. Even with all of the coffee she consumed she was still ready for sleep.

She climbed into bed and was asleep before too long. She was awakened a couple of hours later with nightmares about zombies. Zombies were trying to get her and the people she was with were too squeamish to kill them. All she knew was that she had to kill them before they bit her and caused her to change into one of them. She sat up and looked around the room and lay back down. She had a difficult time falling back to sleep and when she finally drifted back to sleep she was right back in the zombie dreams again trying to kill zombies. She didn't know where these dreams came from because she didn't even watch zombie movies and she didn't have any kind of fascination with zombies or vampires or any of the usual horror movie creatures.

She woke up at 5:30am and got to work early as usual. Debbie arrived at the last minute like she did the last two days. She got through the day and learned a little and got a bit of experience doing what she was being trained to do. She Received shipments, paid for orders and placed new orders. She rang up customers orders and did a little inventory assessment. She was feeling a little overwhelmed but with Debbie there to walk her through everything she knew she was going to be alright. She went to church that evening but rushed out after the service was over so that she could get home and get in bed. She was having a difficult time getting accustomed to the new schedule. It's only been 3 days, I will get used to it she told herself. She made it through the first week. Friday morning she got up bright and early as per the new schedule and she didn't get off work until 2pm which meant that she had to hurry and get home to change her clothes and get ready for her counseling appointment with Sara.

She got home at 2:30 that Friday afternoon. She was so beat she just wanted to take a nap. No time for a nap so she made a pot of coffee instead. She washed her face and hands then changed her clothes as quickly as she could. She didn't want to go in her uniform so she made sure her jeans and blouse were already laid out when she got home. She fixed her strong cup of coffee and was thinking of purchasing a cappuccino machine with her next paycheck or maybe she would just do espresso shooters. She needed something to wake her up and keep her moving. She knew it wouldn't be so bad once she got used to the new job duties because learning new stuff is mentally exhausting.

She sat there at the dining table and sipped on her third cup of coffee while she waited for Reverend Joe to arrive. He finally got there about 3:30 and she invited him in. He stepped inside. It smelled of coffee and he took a deep breath inhaling the aroma. Raylynn handed him the to-go mug and he fixed himself a cup of coffee. He looked at the dark color and said you must be tired, I think this is the darkest you have ever made the coffee. He took a sip and almost choked on it. Ray this is some strong coffee he said as he added a little more cream and sugar to the cup of very strong coffee. She gathered her things and they walked out the door, Raylynn locked up as they left.

They shared a little small talk on their way to the clinic and Raylynn told him about the job. It will get better he said reassuringly. I know it's just the learning curve that is the hard part; she said then curled her lip in discontent. When they arrived at the clinic she checked in and Joe selected their seat near the door that lead to the back offices. A few minutes later Sara called her name. She got up and walked back to Sara's office and waited for Sara to unlock the door. They went inside and Raylynn sat down where she usually sat, across from Sara. Sara sat down and opened the file. Raylynn felt like there was a knot in her stomach and she didn't know if it was from the coffee or her emotions.

She knew it wasn't going to be smooth and easy because she knew she had work to do on herself. This was all about changing the way her mind worked and how she responded to everything that was happening in her life. She knew that her brain was wired a long time ago when her parents first started what they did to her. The abuse, the molestation, and the negative responses from her mother instead of her mother helping her and protecting her from that monster who was also her father. She let him do it and then placed the blame on little Raylynn. She put the responsibility of the molestation by her father on the little girl as if she asked for it and was supposed to accept it. She was treated as though that was the reason she was born. All of the abuse in her childhood wired her to accept the way bad people wanted to treat her as if it were normal. Raylynn knew this and she was angry with her parents for starting the whole mess and for creating the secrets that should have been exposed when they happened or better yet should have never happened at all.

She was angry because she was not taught to watch out for the red flags of abusers and instead was taught to conceal what her abusers have done to her. Her life was based on the belief that she was born to be abused and she was supposed to protect the abuser and not herself. How backwards and crazy that sounded yet it was her real life. She told Sara how angry she felt and how she wanted to make all of her abusers pay for what they have done to her and wondered how she could ever get past it. She explained to Sara how the lifetime of abuse has made her feel and how she knew it all began with her parents. It all began with the protection of her abuser instead of protecting her. She allowed others to abuse her because of it. How she was beginning to hate her parents but still couldn't give them up and she felt angry with herself because she couldn't let them go. She spent time wishing they would just die and other times she just wished they were normal parents and that she would have had a normal life.

She asked Sara, "How am I supposed to get passed all of the anger and all that has been done to me"? Sara explained that when the time comes to forgive she will know it and that is when she will get past the anger. I hate feeling this way all of the time, she cried. I don't want to become an angry and bitter old woman who can't live with the past, she explained. Sara listened with compassion but didn't speak, she just allowed Raylynn to talk about how she was feeling. I feel like a failure because I can't get past it and I didn't do anything to protect myself when these things were happening to me. I know why I didn't tell after I was raped, she said but I don't understand it. Why do I hang on to my parents when I detest what they did to me? I know what they did and I still talk to them and deal with their attitude toward me like I was supposed to accept it.

Raylynn talked for a few minutes about how stressed out she gets and how the anxiety affects her physically. She couldn't stand to be where she is in her life at the moment as far as the abuse and the anger she had positive things happening such as the promotion she felt that the anger will hold her back and keep her from moving forward. Sara explained that it is important to allow herself to feel the anger and give it some time. She explained that it was part of the healing process and that healing takes time and that included getting past the anger issues. Raylynn understood that it was part of the healing process but she was afraid she was going to get stuck there in the anger. She was afraid she wouldn't get past it and would be left with nothing but bitterness trapped in the past. She wanted to get past it tomorrow. Sara continued to explain that even molesters have often started out being molested that abusers were often created by being abused. We learn from our experiences and sometimes people become what have happened to them.

Raylynn thought about what she had said about the abusers being abused and she knew that her parents grew up being abused as children and that they must have learned the behavior from their parents who may have learned it from theirs. Maybe she knew because she has always known that is the reason she doesn't want to give up her parents. Maybe she feels sorry for them. Maybe she does have a little bit of compassion for them but she still feels angry about what they did to her. She felt that they ruined her and left her to pick up the pieces and at the same time she didn't believe that they wanted to ruin her that it wasn't what her parents had intended it is just what happened.

Maybe it was just the sad part of their own abuse that they learned to be the abusers. I wouldn't put it past their parents to have done the same thing to her parents in about the same way. Parents sometimes treat their own children with the disrespect for humanity that they were brought up with. That thought brought back the poem she had written so long ago. It is about her abusers and rapists. She called it The Cesspool of Humanity. It talked about how they tried to keep her down and keep her in the crap of life. They wouldn't let her get out of the cesspool. She tried to remember how the poem read but she couldn't remember the order of the words at that moment. Just then as she was lost in thought, Sara brought her back to the conversation. What are you thinking about Raylynn, she asked. Just thinking about an old poem I had written a long time ago, Raylynn replied. She told Sara what the poem was about and Sara seemed to understand.

They talked about how she felt so trapped in the crap of life even when good things were happening all around her. She couldn't seem to get past the abuse and the rapes. She couldn't seem to get past the beatings in her marriage. Sara told her that she believes that it is possible to get past it and to move beyond the abuse. It is possible to get beyond just going through the motions and it is possible to get to a place to forgive.

Raylynn thought for moment that maybe she doesn't want to forgive them and that is why she isn't able to do it. She is not at a place to want to do it. She hated feeling angry but maybe she wanted to feel angry deep down inside she knew that maybe just maybe she wanted to hate them. She tried to explain that to Sara who seemed to understand her ramblings. It's time to end here Sara said. We can talk some more of where you are at next week and see where you are then. They ended there and walked out to the waiting room where Reverend Joe was waiting for her. They said goodbye and Raylynn walked over to Joe and said well, lets get out of here. Joe said okay Ray; let's go get something to eat. They went to their usual place; Jim's Burgers and got their usual meal of bacon cheese burgers and a frozen cola. They talked for awhile about this and that then Joe asked her about the meditation class.

Are you going to be ready in the spring for the meditation class? He asked patiently. I think so Joe. It depends on my work hours and what time the meditation classes will be held. I think if we do it about 7pm I should be able to make it. I have to work until 6pm every night and I have Sunday off, she said. Well I think you should give Reverend Charlene a call and discuss the details and do it soon so that she can plan and schedule the classes between the other classes that are going on in the church. She has to make sure it doesn't overlap with another class that is using the space.

I will give her a call Joe, she said. Oh, I need her number do you have it? She asked. Joe gave her Reverend Charlene's cell number and left it at that. He knew she would call her; Raylynn always came through with what she said she would do. They sat and visited with one another for a little while longer then headed back to her place. Raylynn really enjoyed visiting with Joe, well for the most part. Sometimes when he pushes her to do something like volunteering she didn't like it so much.

They got back to her place and he walked her to the door. You are a good person Ray, don't forget that. You have a lot to offer the world and you will be a great assistant manager, then he said goodbye. Raylynn walked into her apartment then sat her things on the sofa. She thought about her meeting with Sara and remembered the poem. She couldn't remember how the poem read so she turned on her computer. I think I saved it on my computer I will give it a look she thought out loud.

When her computer was finally ready she sat down in front of it and searched for her poem. She found it a few minutes later. She read it out loud.

Cesspool
You were bad, I was good
In a cesspool there you stood
Your hand held out, asked for help
Lured me in without a doubt
I grabbed your hand, you pulled me in
you held me down, I could not win
To get out, I tried so hard
Because of you, my life is scarred
It took me years to find the key
from your clutches I broke free
Here I am, doing well
You can go live in hell
All you are we plainly see
in the cesspool of humanity

How she wanted to break free from the anger she felt inside. She wanted to break free from the trap of all that once was and move on to what can be.

Chapter 11

Dealing with Anger

The next few weeks went by without much change and Raylynn thought she was going to just grow to be a bitter old woman who could never have a relationship. How would she ever be able to find forgiveness? How will she be able to forgive herself for allowing these things to happen to her or to forgive the abusers and rapists? Being able to forgive would be better. She found that she imagined that her abusers were all beheaded with their heads rolling around in a basket. What would it be like to see them all beheaded, would that make things better? Would I feel better if that happened? She asked herself. She didn't see how that would make her feel better and she knew she would first have to forgive herself for not fighting back and for not reporting the abuse and the rapes. She knew that she was rewired not to tell when she was very young and had to find a way to forgive. She knew it would be better if they simply didn't matter any more.

She spent thc last few weeks feeling the anger and allowing herself to be angry at her abusers and she knew that eventually they wouldn't matter anymore. The dreams have shifted and she is now dreaming that she is winning the battles most of the time. Between zombie dreams where she is killing zombies to beating up the monsters and winning with her will power she is having less dreams about being chased by bad guys. She doesn't know what caused the change but she knew the change is taking place. She thought for a while at looking at them as the damaged people they are and thought perhaps viewing them as weak and damaged themselves such as looking at the abuse they endured and seeing that their abuse damaged them and rewired their minds to think the way they do that would cause them to commit the crimes they have committed.

A child who is abused will sometimes turn into the abuser as they grow up. A child molester has often been molested. She knew that both of her parents are victims of heinous abuse in their childhoods which is likely why they abused her, she thought. Her mother who was a victim of her mother and Raylynn's father who was a victim of his father's cruel abuse made him the way he is. They were both victims of abuse. They were once helpless and defenseless children who abused by their parents in some of the most intolerable ways to abuse a child. She recalled her father's near death experiences from his alcoholic father while her mother suffered at the hands of her parents in much of the same way she treated Raylynn.

Raylynn recalled her grandmother's cruel nature and hatefulness toward both Raylynn and her mother. I wonder if my grandmother was a victim of such abuse or did it start with my grandmother, she thought. She thought long and hard over the past three weeks or so about her parents and her grandparents. Sometimes a child can have the best parents and still turn out to become a drug addict or alcoholic, she thought as the days went by. If she can just get past her parents abuse and forgive them then she will be able to move on to forgiving the next one and then the next one. She made her goal to work through the feelings of each individual monster.

She was doing well with her new job position and was starting to get used to it. She continued to see Reverend Joe on Tuesday evenings instead of Wednesday and was still able to attend both Wednesday and Sunday services. She spent a lot of time talking to Joe and they often talked about the horrible things she would like to do to those who have hurt her so badly. They always ended up joking and laughing about it. It seemed to help Raylynn to joke about how she would like to shoot them in the kneecaps or break their arms so they couldn't do it to someone else. She and Sara often talked about how she felt about them getting away with what they did. Raylynn told Sara she would like to see them all exposed for what they are and for them to lose any social support they may have. She often thought that she would feel avenged if everyone knew what they have done and everyone walked away from them and turned their backs on them so they have no outside strength to lean on.

She knew that if she told everyone they would either not care or just not believe her and she had to find it within herself to not care about that anymore. In one of her counseling sessions with Sara, she had told Sara that she knew that if she was not bothered by what they had done and it no longer held her back and she had a successful life; they would be most angry indeed.

Sara suggested that she keep a journal and try to write down everything she was feeling and what she was thinking about. She found that 3 weeks later although she was still feeling angry she was feeling less angry. It was now Tuesday and her shift was almost over. She thought about seeing Joe and how much fun she has been having with him the last few weeks. She couldn't wait to get off of work to see him. She actually felt that Joe was becoming an even closer friend than Sandra and maybe even her best friend.

As the time crept by, her anticipation to see Joe increased. 5pm finally made its turn around the clock and hurriedly finished writing her product orders to be called in tomorrow. She found that it was a lot easier to complete her inventory count a day early so she knew what she needed and can fill out the order form a day ahead. She quickly said goodbye then headed to the Dark Roast. She arrived at the dark roast in her uniform at the same time as Reverend Joe. She parked across the parking lot from him. They walked into the little coffee shop together then Raylynn excused herself to go wash her face and hands. She just felt better if she washed up after work. There was so much dirt and dust at work and she had to touch so much of the supplies and goods to clean, count and straighten up that she always got dirty. Raylynn hated to feel the grit from the dirt on her hands and face.

She finished up in the ladies room then walked out to see Joe sitting at a table near the window with two cups of hot coffee and a pile of cream and sugar. Raylynn walked over and sat down. How have you been doing? He asked as he stirred his coffee. Fine, she replied. I have decided to work on forgiving my parents first then I will worry about the others. I think doing that will be more helpful. Just take it one abuser at a time. After all everything is as we perceive it to be, she said confidently. If you think you are ready for that than I say go for it. There is no rush. If you need to feel angry let yourself feel it but when you are done with it and are ready to forgive and let go then I say go for it, he said as reassuringly as he could.

I'm tired of feeling angry with them all. I am ready for them all to just not matter any more. I just want to be able to go on with my life and be happy. I am sick and tired of the anxiety and the anger. I'm so tired of feeling so negatively about it. I have to find a way to let it go, she said. She has forgiven her last husband but can't seem to find the reserve to forgive her last boyfriend, the one who raped her. She feels so angry that she wishes he would suffer. She wants him to suffer. I know that I will be in a good place if I can think about him and not wish for him to be punished. When his punishment doesn't matter to me anymore, she said to Joe who was now standing by the girl behind the counter. Go find us a seat Ray and I will be right there with our order.

He brought the tray with sandwiches to the table and lowered the tray so that Raylynn can pick up her sandwich. He placed his sandwich on the table in front of him then put the tray in the rack over the trash can. As he walked back to the table he noticed Raylynn seemed to be a little stressed out. He noticed it more when she didn't know he was looking at her. He sat down at the table and asked what she was so stressed out about. She looked at him with a shocked expression. Is it that obvious? She said. Well yeah and I know you well enough to know when something is bothering you, he replied.

I am just a little stressed out about how I am feeling about all of this and wondering if the anger is ever going to leave me alone. I understand how you are feeling Ray, but worrying about it is not going to help. Just relax and let it happen. Everything has to take its course and it will eventually happen Ray, I promise. You have already begun your journey on your road to healing. Just keep up what you are doing Ray and you will make it through, you will see, he said softly. He had such a kind way about him and the way he said things to her made her feel so much better and she actually felt better after talking to him about the things she would like to happen to all of her abusers. She feels better when they end with jokes about them. They talked more about how she felt and like usual they ended up with the jokes and Reverend Joe had her laughing so hard her sides ached and her cheeks were cramping from smiling.

With Yule only being a little over a week away, they made plans to spend the whole Yule day together. Raylynn invited him to her apartment and she was going to cook a nice Yule dinner. Instead of turkey or ham she decided to make a roasted chicken with traditional sides. Since they went to Sandra's for thanksgiving which was most uncomfortable but brought them closer together, he has yet to sample her cooking. He heard from Gerty and Rose that she was an amazing cook and he was dying to find out. He loved to eat good food which was his weakness. She was going to make some homemade rolls, breads and pie. She can make the most delicious pumpkin pie they claimed. The two old women were busy playing matchmaker with Reverend Joe and Raylynn. They felt these two would be a good match. Reverend Joe knew they were meddling but didn't mind because he already had an interest in Raylynn and were glad that these women agreed with it.

Several of the church members have been discussing the needs of Reverend Joe and a woman's touch is one of the few needs that have yet to be met. They know how much time he donates to the shelter and to the community as well as the church and they know he isn't eating right at all. They suspect that the nearest to a decent meal he eats is when he gets a sandwich with Raylynn and if they were to become personally involved it would do both of them some good. Sandra suggested that Raylynn invite him to Yule dinner and do something special since they are both alone. A few of the other church members have been hinting to Raylynn to cook a few meals for him and maybe offer to spend a little more time with him or help him around his house.

Raylynn didn't know what to think of the boldness of these members who think that she should offer to tidy his house or cook him some meals. She really liked him but she didn't know if she should try to make any moves on him considering her situation with counseling and how she feels about relationships at the moment. What if she starts to have a relationship with him and then she realizes that she can't commit especially with how angry she is at her abusers who were mostly male. She doesn't hate men and she definitely doesn't hate Joe but she is afraid that her anger will be misguided and she may take out some of it on him. Besides, what if he doesn't like her the same way? If he doesn't like her the same way any attempt to move into his life could chase him away and she liked the way things were. She liked being able to meet with him a couple times a week and just talk about stuff. She likes hearing his stories about the shelter and she needs him. She needs someone to lean on when the days are at their toughest with everything. Reverend Joe often tells the old women to mind their own business but follows it with a chuckle. The others in the church can see the affections between the two and they are already aware of the feelings between them but the two don't have a clue about the others feelings.

They gently nudge them closer together and the two are often very shy and don't want to rush into anything. The church wants to see them have a spring wedding but if they don't start budging the church will be absent the blessed ceremony come spring. Raylynn sat there at the table in the little Coffee house watching Joe talk. She tried to imagine what it was going to be like on Yule. She wondered what she should get him for a gift. With her new pay raise she could get him something nice she thought.

Joe, can I ask you something? She said sheepishly. Sure Ray, what's up? He replied. What would you like for Yule? She asked shyly. Um, do you mean for dinner? He asked. No silly, I mean for a gift. I want to get you something but I am not sure what you would like or what you need. Oh Ray, that is very thoughtful but you don't need to get me anything, really, he said with a smile. I want to get you something. I want to give you something because you have already done so much for me. It would make me happy, she said, batting her eyelashes and giving him a sweet smile. I don't know Ray, I guess I could use a watch to keep me on time or a nice book to read when I am alone and bored but most of all I could use a close friend like you to keep me company on Yule, he said smartly.

Joe, I will find something for you, something you can use. I won't spend too much I promise but it will be something sweet and useful. If I get you a book what type of books do you like to read? She asked. Well, I have always enjoyed a nice mystery novel; you know something to keep me in suspense. She thought about a book but she really wanted to get him something special. She decided she would go shopping and see what she could afford. She already had $50 saved back and she would have another $50 that she could spend. She sat there day dreaming about it. He sat across from her at the table and just watched her as she got lost in her thoughts. It was getting late and he had to get home to prepare for the morning. He had to be at work early in the morning around 8am and didn't want to forget anything. He also had to finish preparing for

Wednesday night. He wanted to talk about the holidays that were coming up and about giving over the holidays. He also knew that Raylynn had to get up early. He cleared his throat to get her attention. She looked up at him and apologized for getting lost in thought once again.

It's okay Ray, I am getting used to it, he said with a chuckle. We should get going Ray, it's getting late. We both have to get up early in the morning, he said as he stood up. He gathered all of the trash at the table and carried it to the trash can. Raylynn stood up and they walked out together. He walked her to her car and said goodnight. Raylynn drove home thinking about what she was going to get Joe for Yule. She decided that Sunday she was going to go shopping. She had two weeks left to shop and she was going to find something good for him. She pulled into the parking lot of her apartment and parked as close to her door as she could. She went inside and locked the door behind her.

She walked into her room and put on her pajamas and got ready for bed. She had a difficult time falling asleep that night because she was so excited about buying a gift for Joe. She doesn't spend time with her parents any more because her mother would often comment that she just wanted something from them is why she came around. She just decided it was best if she didn't impose on them. She wished she could have regular parents who loved her and wanted her around and who would care about her enough to be concerned for her welfare and who didn't abuse her when she was growing up. She wished she had a loving family. She was always the outcast with her cousins and they often teased her while growing up. She hated her cousins for being so cruel and made sure she never had any interactions with them now that she was grown.

She finally drifted off to sleep. She had a fabulous dream about the moon that night. She dreamed she took a trip to the moon with a group of friends and they got to eat all kinds of delicious food. She also dreamed that she was staring up at the stars and the earth while lying on her back on a blow up sofa on the moon. She went down a long flight of stairs and was wearing fabulous clothes. Her dreams were strange and wonderful all at the same time. She didn't know why she was having those dreams but it was wonderful not to dream about killers and violence. It was delightful to dream something strange instead of frightening. Her alarm went off and it was still dark outside.

All she wanted was to lay back down and go back to sleep. She knew she couldn't do that. She had to get up and get moving. She went to the kitchen and made a pot of coffee as usual then got her shower and got ready for work. Wednesday went by just as quickly at night and before she knew it she had to be at the church for Wednesday night services. She loved going to the little church with all the people there to talk to. She wasn't alone any more she realized as she walked through the door. She had her church to spend time with and she was sure that if she really needed anything her church would be there to help her if they could.

They all made her feel so warm and welcomed. She was thankful for such a wonderful friend like

Sandra. Sandra spent months dragging Raylynn around from group to group so everyone got to know Raylynn so even on the days that Sandra wasn't there Raylynn was and people came up to her and started talking to her. She often had a difficult time getting out of there after church and found herself very tired the next morning before going to work so early. She knew she couldn't have it all her way. She had to get up early to have this job and the extra hours were nice on the paycheck.

Friday arrived before she knew it and she sat there after work drinking her coffee while waiting for Reverend Joe to arrive. She thought about how she has been feeling about her abusers. She has been working on how she feels about her parents and how they have behaved all of these years. She thought about how they were abused by their parents and how similar the abuse was that she endured over her childhood. She realized she couldn't hate her parents and was finding that she was not as angry with her parents as she was even last week. The anger seemed to be subsiding. Other than picturing her father's head rolling in a basket a couple of weeks ago she really didn't have that much anger toward them. She realized they were victims too. It is hard to hate someone who was a victim no matter what they have done.

They didn't mean to destroy me she thought. They just did it because that is all they knew she told herself. What they have done is wrong but they were wronged when they were growing up and just did the same as their parents. She listened to her parents' stories and to her aunts and uncles when they told their stories as she was growing up. They grew up during a time when women didn't work but they stayed home and took care of the household while the men were allowed to do as they pleased because they worked hard to support the family. Their mothers allowed their fathers to abuse them. After all what choice did they have? She sat there thinking about how she was feeling when she thought about her parents.

She actually felt sorry for them and knew that what they had done was not her fault. It had nothing to do with her. They did what they did because of them and what happened to them as children. She knew she would never allow her parents around any children that may ever be in her care. They would not be allowed because they can't help themselves and they have chosen to become the abusers. She felt that she was making progress because when she thought about her parents she didn't feel the anger swell up inside her like it once had. She didn't want to get even and she didn't care if they were punished any more. She felt they were punishing themselves and that is what she found to be the most amazing part. She didn't care. It didn't matter any more. She would work on her next abusers and try to get to a point to genuinely not care if they are punished or not.

She knew she could never let them back into her life, just because she forgives them does not mean they can come back into her life to abuse her more. She had to keep them out of her life to protect herself from being hurt any more. Just as she finished with her second cup of coffee, Reverend Joe knocked on her door. She got up and opened the door and there he stood with a beautiful evergreen tree in his hands. It was a potted tree so it's life would not be wasted. She was amazed at how good the tree smelled and was grateful that he brought it for her. I thought we could decorate it together he said as he sat it down in her living room.

I love that idea Joe, she said as she walked around the tree. It is perfect and beautiful, I love it. I don't have any decorations for a tree though. I usually put up my tiny tree that is already decorated, she said as she pointed to a tiny box next to the television. That's okay Ray, we can go get some decorations after you talk to Sara, he said cheerfully. We can sit it right here next to the television as he sat it down. What do you think Ray? He asked happily. I love it there. I don't watch television often anyway, she replied. Well, we should be getting out of here Joe, she said. Would you like a cup of coffee before we go? Sure Ray that would be great, he said. She handed him the to-go mug full of hot coffee. He managed to prepare his cup of coffee then they headed out the door. It was a rainy day and quite wet outside but Ray didn't mind and she thought, besides it isn't raining at the moment. What a great day this is she thought as she walked out the door. She turned and looked at the tree one last time before she closed and locked the door.

They walked to Joe's car and he opened the door and helped her climb in. He hurried around to the other side and got in the car. His heater didn't work in his beat up old car but Ray didn't mind. She had her toasty warm jacket and mittens to keep her warm. They headed over to the clinic. I want to buy the decorations, okay Joe, she said. He politely agreed to let her buy the decorations for the tree to make her happy. He knew she wouldn't be happy unless she paid for them. The decorations are all yours Ray, he said with a smile.

They arrived at the clinic right on time. They walked inside and Raylynn checked in while Reverend Joe found them a seat near the door to the back offices. Sara was always prompt to call her name and rarely went over the time allowed. They engaged with regular chatter as they walked back to her office. Sara opened the door to her office and Raylynn stepped through the door. She sat down in her usual place at the little round table and waited for Sara to get comfortable. Once Sara was seated she opened the file and asked Raylynn how she had been doing. I have been doing pretty good, she replied. I haven't had as many bad dreams lately and in fact I have been having simple weird dreams about aliens and the moon and strange things such as that, Raylynn said as she twisted in her seat. What about the anxiety? Sara asked. Well, I still have anxiety and am still trying to get past that. I have been trying to get past it for awhile now. They discussed the anxiety such as how she felt during an anxiety attack and what she had experienced.

I think we should try an exercise with meditation to try and help the anxiety, Sara suggested. Sara explained in detail how to try to use the meditation so that she could overcome the anxiety. Raylynn explained that she already uses cleansing breaths to get through the anxiety attacks and that it seemed to help. Raylynn agreed to work through it with the meditation by putting herself there in the happy place that she created with the waterfall and the sound of the river and all of the fresh outdoor smells. Raylynn knew she couldn't spend a lot of time at work doing a meditation every time she had an anxiety attack but she could continue with the cleansing breaths for the emergency and then excuse herself to meditate to go finish the meditation and calm down. She was pretty good at getting through them already since she started meditating a few months ago and the cleansing breaths seem to help to get things under control so that she could move on through her work day.

It is not always convenient to stop and put herself into the happy waterfall place but she would definitely try. Raylynn talked about how she doesn't feel angry about her parents anymore but the others she is very angry about what they have done. She worked through it with her parents and that is all the farther she has gotten with her parents. She didn't care if they ever were punished because she felt they were already being punished with life circumstances. She talked about how she felt about her parents and that she seen them for the victims that they are that made them the way they are today.

Raylynn spent the rest of the session talking about how she felt about the others, about her ex husbands and boyfriend who abused her. She told Sara that she was angry with herself for allowing them to abuse her.

She didn't call the police to tell what they had done. She was angry that she let them get away with it. She was so frustrated with herself for not letting herself do what she should have done and turned them all in.

Time went by very quickly and it was time to end the session before she knew it. Sara closed the file and they walked out to the waiting room where Joe was sitting. They said goodbye and Raylynn walked over to Joe as he stood up and they walked out together.

Raylynn was feeling a little overwhelmed by all the feelings they talked about in the session and decided now would be a great time to do a quick meditation. She told Joe she was going to get grounded and just give her a minute. They got in the car and Joe sat there in silence as Raylynn took her cleansing breath and visualized her happy place. Once she had finished she felt a lot better and could enjoy their shopping for decorations.

She looked at Joe who seemed to be meditating a little too. He took a deep breath and looked at her and smiled. We are going to be just fine Raylynn, just fine, he said quietly. As she looked at him she smiled and giggled a little. He started the car and they were on their way. Are you hungry Ray? He asked. Naw, not right now, I really just want to go shopping for decorations. I can throw something together at home for us if you want to stay for dinner then help me decorate that beautiful tree you brought over, she said happily. Um, sure Ray I would love to do that. Where do you want to go for the decorations? He asked. Oh, how about, Shagways discount store. I think that would be a great place to start. Shagways discount store was a little shop that offered off brand items at a very low price. She loved that store because she could get all kinds stuff for less. It made her shopping trips all that much better. They used to have clothes but they haven't had clothes in some time now.

They arrived at Shagways in no time at all. They went inside and Raylynn picked out some of the decorations. They purchased tinsel and some glass balls as well as some plastic gingerbread men and two boxes of lights. They picked a beautiful red topper that was laced with glitter. This is going to be the most beautiful tree alive. She was so happy about the decorations that she bounced with every step. They checked out and went to her place. The store was not far from her house so they were home in just a few minutes. They walked up to Raylynn's apartment and just as Raylynn was unlocking the door, Barbara came bouncing down the stairs. Hi Ray, she said as she approached them. Hi Barbara, Raylynn replied.

Barbara introduced herself to Reverend Joe and gave Raylynn a wink. Raylynn introduced Joe to Barbara. This is one of the Clergy of our church, we call him Reverend Joe, Raylynn said with pride. He brought me a Christmas tree earlier and we are just getting back from shopping, she said. Oh well that's nice Barbara responded as if she didn't know about the tree. Barbara knew everything that happened in the apartment complex. Well, we need to get busy, see you later Barbara, Raylynn said kindly then stepped inside her apartment and Joe followed behind her. Joe closed the door behind him and sat the bags of decorations next to the tree. Raylynn walked into the kitchen and began to pull food out of the cupboards and refrigerator. She decided to make her favorite meal, Fried Chicken, corn and mashed potatoes. She didn't eat this meal very often but it was her favorite.

Reverend Joe walked into the kitchen and asked if she needed any help. She quickly put him to work peeling potatoes. He was happy to do it. He liked the idea of them cooking together. This is the first meal you have cooked for me, he said as he peeled potatoes. He teased a little as he worked. She responded with a chuckle. They had a good time cooking dinner together, they laughed and they talked about non-important things and talking about them seemed to be just as important as the important things in life. Reverend Joe stood in the kitchen under foot while Raylynn prepared the meal. Joe inhaled deeply and said it smells delicious; I can't wait to taste it. It's almost finished she replied. We will be eating soon. It only took Raylynn 45 minutes to prepare the meal and have it on the table ready to eat. He was very impressed. They sat down to the table and ate their dinner; Talking as usual.

Later they decorated the tree. Raylynn was happy to have the company. She couldn't remember when was the last time she had so much fun. She hung a candy cane just as he leaned close to her to hang an ornament high on the tree. She could smell his cologne. She never really got that close to him before and his smell made her weak in the knees. She instinctively pulled away from him and she felt a little flushed. After the tree was decorated they stepped back and took a look at it. They both nodded with approval at a job well done. Reverend Joe looked at Raylynn and said I have to get going Ray; I have to be at the Shelter early tomorrow. He took his leave about 8:30 and Raylynn knew she had to get up early tomorrow too. She locked the door behind him and walked into her room and fell back on her bed.

She sighed with contentment as she laid there thinking about how much fun she had with Joe. She laid there for a few minutes longer then got ready for bed. She slept well that night and woke up feeling refreshed in the morning. She had a few strange dreams about a childhood friend. She dreamed that her childhood friend Cindy, who was a child in her dream, was taking pills and Raylynn had to stop her. She welcomed the strange dreams because they were better than the nightmares that disturbed her sleep. She all too often woke from the tormenting dreams but not lately and she was happy with it.

Chapter 12

Yule Tidings and Holiday Cheer

Yule was just days away and Raylynn had to make sure she had all the food she wanted to make for Yule dinner. It should be special and with candles she thought to herself. It should have some decorations and a tablecloth to liven the scene. She had a few extra dollars left over and she wanted to go shopping. She wanted to get Joe that watch she seen the other day at the little shop around the corner. She picked up her purse and walked out the door with purpose. Shopping was going to be fun. She was looking forward to cooking and she liked the idea of giving a gift. She arrived at the little shop around the corner in just minutes.

She found a parking place close to the door and went inside. She looked around the little shop and there was all sorts of jewelry. She looked in the cases at the different shiny necklaces, bracelets and rings. Some were absolutely stunning while others were big and gaudy, some were right down ugly. The salesman approached her and calmly asked; may I help you? Raylynn looked up at him to see him smiling at her with his hands clasped in front of him. Um, yes, I am looking for a man's watch. I am giving it to a friend for Yule and I want it to be special but not too expensive. He gave her a knowing look and said I have a collection you might find meets your needs right over here then he motioned to a small case off to the side full of watches.

They walked over to the small case and Raylynn seen that they were nice watches. They were cheaper than the other watches in the big case in the front but they looked durable and attractive. She looked them over and decided on the one at the top. It looked like it had a diamond in the 12 O'clock position. She asked to see it and the salesman pleasantly took the watch out and handed it to her. She looked it over and asked if that was a real diamond pointing at the little shiny sparkle at the top. Oh no, it isn't a real diamond but it really is a nice looking watch. It has a one year warranty and comes with this nice case, the salesman said. She looked at the other watches again and decided that this was the watch she was going to buy. She knew he needed one because he has replaced his $7.00 watch several times and she knew he needed a nice one to wear with his suit on Sunday and Wednesday night. He was such a strange man sometimes when it came to things he needed.

She purchased the watch and it was only $50.00. She took her purchase and carefully put it in her purse then walked out of the shop. She got in her car and headed toward the grocery store. She got in and out of the grocery store without any problems. The store had everything she needed for dinner. She took a vacation day off from work that Yule and made sure her shift was properly covered. She would work Christmas for sure but Yule this year was a special occasion. Steve didn't mind her taking off a few days before Christmas since she was going to work Christmas. She switched shifts with Cassy on Sunday and Cassy was pleased to have Christmas off. Raylynn and Steve Usually worked Christmas together and she never took off for Yule but this year was different. This year she had someone to spend it with she thought fondly.

She spent her day off shopping and putting away the food. She also took the time to wrap Joe's gift. She had been feeling a little more cheery lately and not just because of the holidays coming up. She was feeling less stressed and was having less anxiety lately. She thought about the last couple of weeks and realized she had significantly less anxiety or so it seemed because she was able to work through the anxiety attacks with ease. She found that the cleansing breaths seemed to really help and she noticed that when some of the abuse memories were triggered she didn't feel so angry about them. She was still very angry about the latest rape but the others she wasn't so upset about. Some of the abuse she didn't feel anything at all and some of her abusers she realized she had forgiven them.

She realized she needed to forgive herself although it wasn't really her fault she seemed to hold a little resentment and anger towards herself for picking the wrong people. She picked people who treated her like her parents did. They didn't have respect for her and she didn't try to make them have respect. She allowed them to treat her badly and for that she was angry with herself most of all. She had to find forgiveness for herself after all she had to live with herself and could avoid the other 3 men who participated in raping her but she could not avoid herself.

When she arrived at home with all of her purchases she began to carry them in slowly. Barbara was just getting home from spending the day out with some friends and seen Raylynn carrying in her groceries. Hey Ray, you want some help with that she squawked as she approached Raylynn. Oh no that's okay Barbara, she said cheerfully as she carried in the last few bags. Barbara followed her back to her car as Raylynn grabbed the last item, her purse with the watch, before locking up the car. The bag was sticking half out of her purse in plain sight. Whatchya got there Ray? She asked as she pointed toward the bag with the watch.

Oh, my friend Reverend Joe is coming over in a few days and I wanted to give him a gift, Raylynn said as she opened the bag for Barbara to see. Barbara peeked in the bag and seen the box. Oh Ray is that jewelry? I bet it's a watch she exclaimed. Can I see what it looks like? She squealed as she clapped her hands and jumped up and down. Sure let's go inside and I will show you what it looks like. They stepped inside the door of her apartment and she took it out of the bag. She sat the bag on the table and opened the box. Oh that is a nice man's watch. Is that a real diamond? Barbara asked as she looked it over. No, No it's not. But it is beautiful and I think the watch will last for a while. Do you think He will like it? Raylynn asked as she carefully caressed the watch. Oh I am sure he will love it. Barbara said with confidence. I know any man would be pleased with it, the watch is beautiful.

I am going to wrap it up as soon as I get my groceries put away. Barbara looked around the room and noticed the tree. Oh I love your beautiful tree Ray. I had seen Reverend Joe bring it over. You did a beautiful job decorating it. Barbara said as she looked it over. Thanks Barbara, Raylynn said. Well, I gotta get my groceries put away before they spoil, she said as she walked Barbara to the door. Okay, I can take a hint, I'm leaving she chuckled as she walked out of the door. Raylynn giggled and closed the door behind her. As much of a pain she is, she is still adorable, she thought as she walked into the kitchen to put the groceries away. She planned to make all kinds of homemade delights over the next few days. She put all of the food in its place then she hurried and got the watch wrapped and placed it under the tree.

Her phone rang in her pocket and she tried to catch the caller in time but failed. It was Joe, She forgot about meeting Joe. She hurriedly called him back. When he answered she began to explain why she wasn't at the Dark Roast. Slow down Ray, it's okay I was just worried about you is all. You have never stood me up before and I was a little concerned. Do you want to cancel and just see you at church? He asked. No, no, no, I will be there shortly, I am on my way she said as she grabbed her jacket and purse and made a dash for the door. It was already 1pm and for the first time she was going to be very late. She drove the quickest route but it was still going to take about 20 minutes to get there. She arrived to see Reverend Joe sitting at a table near the window. They caught eyes and she gave him a sheepish smile.

Once inside as she approached Reverend Joe she had seen that he had two cups of coffee and two sandwiches sitting on the table in front of him. She sat down and said once again that she was sorry for being late. I got you something good Joe, what I have been wanting to get you, something you can use, she said. It's okay Ray, don't feel bad and I appreciate the gift, I am sure it is very nice, he said then he took a bite of his sandwich. She added cream and sugar to her coffee then took a bite of her sandwich. She slowly chewed her bite then said thank you Joe for being so understanding. Not many people in my life have been as understanding as you. He waved his hand in the air and said, I care about you Ray, which is what people do when they care about someone, they try to understand when things don't always go the way we want them to go, and then he gave her a smile that made her melt. She blushed at the mere thought of the melting feeling she got when he smiled at her. She took another bite of her sandwich then a sip of her coffee.

He is so perfect she thought to herself. He does everything right. He seems to never be a jerk and never seems to get mad at me even when I deserve it. Her mind drifted off on how wonderful he always was. If she only knew that it would stay this perfect she would try to find out if he liked her in the same way. She has had lots of people tell her they cared about her and then either walked all over her or walked out. She knew that sometimes people say they care when they don't really care that much but Joe was always so nice and he seemed to really care. Before she knew it, Joe was waving his hand in front of her face. Ray, are you there? He asked. She quickly came back to reality. Where were you? He asked with concern. Oh, I was just lost in thought is all. I'm sorry, I don't mean to ignore you but I was thinking about something you had said. She replied.

Alright Ray, I really need you to stay with me when we are visiting. He said sternly. They finished their lunch and visited a while. Raylynn fought with her mind's desire to wander. She didn't know why she couldn't stay focused. She could only guess why and she thought it may be because of all of the excitement over the next few days. She has a lot to do and little time to do it. She is planning to make her famous pumpkin bread for Joe and some Pumpkin cookies and more. She really enjoyed her time spent with Joe and she wanted to treat him to a truly special meal.

Well Ray, I need to go prepare for the Sunday night sermon, He said. It was almost 3:30 when they parted and Raylynn wanted to make at least one loaf of pumpkin bread before church. She arrived at home about 4pm. After she unlocked the door and walked in she immediately sat her purse on the table and hung up her coat. She then walked into the kitchen and washed her hands in preparation to make the pumpkin bread. She wanted to send a whole loaf home with Joe which meant she needed two loaves. She got the loaf of pumpkin bread in the oven to bake and she put the second loaf in the crock pot to cook. She loved breads cooked in the crock pot and she figured pumpkin bread would be amazing if cooked in the crock pot. She wanted to see which one was better.

She walked into her room and put on her dress pantyhose and shoes then walked into the bathroom and brushed her long hair. She decided to pull her hair up into a bun for church and figured it would be best if her hair was up out of the way when she finished the bread. She could smell the spices of the bread throughout her apartment and she just had to try a piece when it was finished. She planned to slice the bread up once it had cooled enough then she wrapped it well and kept it in the refrigerator. She thought it was the perfect plan to have it ready for Yule and sneak a piece today. She often was careful of what she ate to be sure to keep her figure thin. She still had a fear of not being able to get away if she needed so she often skipped meals and avoided snacks. This year was going to be different. This year she was going to pig out for Yule and have a bite of everything.

The winter solstice was one of her favorite celebrations when she has someone to share it with. She loves all of the festivities and parties this time of year. She usually got invited to someone's party but this year she didn't get any invites but it was just fine because she was going to spend the holiday with Joe.

That night at church Reverend Joe gave the best sermon. He told the story of Yule and he made it so exciting that it kept everyone on the edge of their seat. Sandra was there as usual and she dragged Raylynn around the room visiting with everyone, gathering up all of the gossip. Raylynn had to excuse herself after a few minutes because she knew she had to get up early and it was already almost 9pm. She got home around 9:25 and went to her room and put on her pajamas. She washed her face and hands and went directly to bed. She was very sleepy and went right to sleep. She got up the next morning feeling refreshed. She didn't have a single nightmare all night long. She got up and got ready for work. She only had two cups of coffee on this Monday morning and still felt fine.

The days have gone by so easily lately and she was getting used to her new schedule. She liked the new girl she hired and had a great time at work. They worked together very well and she knew life was going to be good. Sure she still had some anxiety and a few flashbacks but life seems to be going pretty darn good for Raylynn. She enjoyed the next couple of days especially visiting Joe at the Dark Roast coffee house. She got some of her sweet treats made and Wednesday night they had a Yule celebration at church. They didn't exchange gifts but they did have a potluck and Joe did a fantastic job at making it enjoyable for everyone. He only spoke a little and was the host of the party but there were so many people there that they had to line the walls with tables for the food and place extra chairs for people to sit.

They had to have it in the main hall which was the biggest room where church services were held. A group of the teens performed a little story of the birth of the Oak King and death of the Holly King and the whole story of winter. It was absolutely amazing and Raylynn enjoyed herself. She didn't get home until 10:30 that night but she didn't care because she was off from work and could sleep in the next day.

Yule morning arrived and Raylynn was so excited. She jumped out of bed by 7am and made a pot of coffee. She pulled out the vanilla flavored creamer to make a special treat for the coffee. She hurried into the shower and washed as quickly as she could. Today was a special day and she had lots to do before Joe arrived at 11am. She quickly put on her nicest pants and blouse then fixed up her hair. She decided to wear makeup on this special day so she spent a few extra minutes doing that. Then she started preparing the sides like green bean casserole and sweet potatoes and other yummy sides. She baked the homemade rolls and set them aside to be warmed as dinner was almost ready.

She had everything prepared all she had to do is cook it all. Joe arrived right on time. He was always predictably on time and she wanted to have a nice lunch prepared for him. She had baked a couple extra rolls and made two sandwiches and had fresh coffee made for him. Joe stepped into her apartment and took a deep sniff. It smells wonderful in here, he said as he looked around. I hope you are hungry because I made us both a sandwich for lunch, she said as she walked to the dining table. I am starved he replied. I thought I would make sure to come hungry so I could try all of your wonderful food, he said happily. I made the roll from scratch, she said as she handed him a plate with the sandwich and a slice of pumpkin bread. Oh, pumpkin bread's my favorite, he said with mouth watering anticipation. They sat at the dining table and ate their lunch.

They were having such a good time just talking and Joe was telling his silly jokes that made Raylynn laugh. After they were done visiting over lunch they went into the living room to exchange gifts. Joe had a small gift bag in his hand and Raylynn picked up the gift she bought for him. She was so excited she couldn't wait to give it to him. Open my gift first Joe, she said as she presented the little wrapped box. He took the little box and he shook it next to his ear. Hmm it doesn't rattle, he said. Then he weighed it in his hand and said it's not too heavy so it isn't a rock. Raylynn growing impatient exclaimed, come on Joe just open it. Joe let out a little giggle then said, okay Ray I'll open it. He carefully took off the paper and then slowly opened the box just a little so he could peak at what was inside. Then he opened the box completely.

It is a very nice watch, he said. Thank you Ray. Try it on Joe, she said excitedly. He took off his beat up little watch and put on the beautiful new watch. Oh that looks very nice on you, she said with a smile. I love it Ray. Here, open your gift now he said as he handed her the little bag. She carefully took out the paper and peered inside the bag. It was a small box inside the little bag. She reached inside the bag and pulled out the box. She looked up at Joe with a sparkle in her eye. She looked back down at the box and opened the little box. It was a beautiful earring and necklace set. That is real amethyst and sterling silver, he said as she pulled them out of the box. She put on the earrings in her pierced ears and asked him to help her put on the necklace. Then she ran into the bathroom to look in the mirror. She wanted to see what she looked like with such beautiful jewelry displayed around her neck. It has been a long time since she has had any jewelry.

She ran back out to the living room and gave Joe a great big hug. Thank you Joe, they are beautiful, I love them! She exclaimed as she hugged him again. He chuckled and said, I'm glad you like them Ray. I knew they would look beautiful on you as soon as I seen them. They sat there in the living room talking about all of their wonderful memories of Past holidays. Joe had many more than Raylynn but she had a few fond memories to look back on. She talked about the time she learned how to make pumpkin bread and he talked about the first time he ever had eaten it. Raylynn learned how to make pumpkin bread in high school. It was her junior year in high school and she was in home economics. Her teacher had this fabulous pumpkin bread recipe and she taught all of her students how to make it for Christmas.

Joe was about six when his grandmother came over for Yule. It was the first year after his grandfather had died so it was a difficult year for the family. She had baked a couple loaves of pumpkin bread because it was his grandfather's favorite breads. She wanted to remember him on the holidays so it became a tradition in his family to have pumpkin bread on Yule. His grandmother continued to bring pumpkin bread on Yule until she passed away during the summer of his 17th birthday. She never remarried and she became the center of the family. It was a sad time when she passed but in remembrance of both of his grandparents his mother began to make pumpkin bread. It wasn't as good as his grandmother's bread but it was still tasty nonetheless. He told her he was glad she knew how to make pumpkin bread and that her pumpkin bread was absolutely delicious. It was lighter in color than his grandmother's but tasted better than his mother's.

Before she knew it, 3pm was already here and she had to start cooking dinner. She put her chicken in the oven and started the potatoes. She put the green bean casserole and sweet potatoes in the oven. She pulled out the pumpkin bread. Her phone rang and she ran to pick it up. It was Sandra. Hi Sandra, Raylynn said as she answered the phone. Hi Ray, I wanted to wish you a happy Yule. Thank you Sandra you are a good friend. I hope you are having a happy Yule as well, Raylynn replied. Tell Reverend Joe I said happy Yule to him too she giggled. Did you open your gifts already? She asked. Yep we did. I gave him a watch and he gave me earrings and a necklace, Raylynn replied. Nice I hope you wear them to church. Has he asked you to be his girlfriend yet? Sandra teased. No silly girl, it isn't like that you know, Raylynn replied as she played with the necklace. Well, I'm going to let you get back to entertaining your guest, she said then said goodbye. Raylynn hung up the phone a little embarrassed from the conversation.

Before long dinner was almost ready. It was time to set the table. She set the places and the candles. She put the cranberry sauce, mixed fruit and breads on the table. Then she took the food out of the oven and set it on the table. She popped the rolls in the oven to warm them a little. Joe, dinner is ready, she called. He got up and walked toward the table. It is beautiful Ray and it smells wonderful, he said. Raylynn handed him the knife and serving fork to cut the chicken to be served. He proudly accepted the job. They had a great dinner and Raylynn pulled out a homemade apple pie. I made this from scratch. I'll warm it in the oven and we can have a piece before you go home.

They had a wonderful day and Raylynn was sorry to see it come to an end. He left about 6:30 with a bunch of leftovers to take home. She had divided up the food in half and made sure he got most of the pumpkin bread. His story was so sweet she couldn't let him go without it. She didn't have counseling tomorrow because it was so close to Christmas and Yule that she decided to take a break and go the following week. She reminded Joe before he left that they don't have counseling and he seemed a little disappointed. She knew that she had made it through the most difficult time of the year. She always felt especially lonely over Christmas and Yule because she didn't have any family to spend it with.

Work kept her busy so she didn't have time to think about it. She was going to work on Christmas which fell on a Sunday this year and she knew she would be tired for church that night. It was going to be okay because Reverend Joe was going to run a movie that night for those who wanted to bring family along. Most had Christian family members so the movie would be one about Santa Claus and the spirit of giving. Sunday was here before she knew it. She had a great time working with Steve again. They didn't have to be there as early as usual and they were closing early that night so Steve and Raylynn Worked together like they usually did.

She didn't get off work until 6pm that night and Steve locked up at 7pm. They weren't going to open again until Raylynn got there at 7am as usual. Since she wasn't having the nightmares she usually had, she didn't seem to need as much sleep. She arrived at church in her uniform because she didn't have time to change. She sat between Sandra and Reverend Joe in the front to watch the movie. It was a really cute movie and there were quite a few people who showed up to watch it. They were each wearing something new. Sandra wanted to see Raylynn's new jewelry and the infamous watch. Everyone showed off their new things and had a fun Christmas night.

Monday things were almost back to normal. They had one more holiday to get past and that was New Year's. Raylynn was going to work New Year's Eve. She was even working a double shift to cover for another employee who wanted off that day. She and Steve worked well together managing the little store and keeping the schedule organized. He was proud of Raylynn for the great job she was doing. He knew when he chose her for the position she was going to do well. He only had to make it through New Year's and He knew the extra pay on Raylynn's paycheck was going to keep her motivated. The year was ending this week and a new one was beginning. It was going to be a new year with Raylynn assisting him.

Chapter 13

Happy New Year's

The last week of the year was going fairly smooth and she hardly gave her ex a single thought. She truly felt happy inside and couldn't wait for New Year's Day. She was going to spend the afternoon with Joe. She didn't realize how much she wanted to spend time with him until she spent Yule with him. She was being drawn to his gentle nature and his kind ways. She found herself thinking about him when she wasn't busy and wasn't quite sure how to think of him at all. She knew he was her friend and that he was different than all of the other men she had ever met but she didn't really know what to think about how she felt about him. She has been wrong before and what if she is wrong now. What if he really isn't such a nice guy and he is just putting up a front to lure her into his evil web?

What if he is really a bad guy pretending to be a good guy like the others have done? Richard pretends to be noble, Jerry pretended to be a nice guy giving gifts and compliments at first, Greg pretended to carry the same ethical beliefs at first, Good ole Dan was the retarded guy and just lied a lot, Even Jack gave good first impressions before he drugged me, she thought. They all were not what they seemed and they all pretended to be something they aren't. Maybe I only see what I want to see and I want to believe that men are nice although they are not. What if Joe only seems to be nice because I want to see him that way? She was afraid to think of him as more than a friend. She was happy with the way things were. He was there, they always had a good time together and things were good between them. She didn't want it to get ruined with the bad stuff. She was afraid to take that chance.

She often thought about what it would be like to have a relationship that was healthy and happy but she didn't really believe that it would ever be real; At least not for her. She had a difficult time believing that she would ever be treated well by anyone in a romantic way. It is better to have friends than it is to be married or even have a boyfriend who will betray me with every chance or worse he will abuse me like the others. I just can't take that chance, at least not right now at this point in my life. I just don't see it happening for me, she thought.

She got focused on the present at that point. She was to meet Joe tonight. It was Tuesday and tonight she was going to meet with him. It is okay to spend so much time with him because he is her friend, she told herself. He is a good friend and time with him is so much fun. She talked herself into feeling justified for the way she felt. She only felt that way because they were friends. She finished her shift and after Steve arrived she was free to go. She said good night and hurried out the door. She went home and washed her face and hands and changed out of her uniform into her jeans. Next week she was going to buy some new jeans and maybe a blouse or two.

For the first time since she has been working at the GoMart she was actually looking forward to her paycheck. She had a little money left over to spend on whatever she wanted and she really wanted to build up her wardrobe. She didn't need expensive things but she was going to buy NEW clothes now instead of shopping at the thrift store. She would shop at the nearby discount clothing stores that have really cute clothes for affordable prices.

She Headed on over to the Dark Roast to meet with Joe. When she arrived she seen him just inside at a table near the window. He always picked a table near the window now that they have been meeting there for months. It was as if he knew her better than she knew herself sometimes. She walked in to see him sitting there with two cups of coffee and two ham and cheese sandwiches on whole wheat bread. She walked over to him and sat down. Hi Joe, she said with a smile. He looked up at her and smiled and said hello back to her. I'm glad you are here, he said in a low tone. You just seen me on Sunday, she said with a giggle. Yeah, but I am glad to see you today Ray, He said sincerely.

What is so special about today? She asked. Oh nothing special about today I guess, he replied. I am just glad to see you today. Friday after you see Sara do you want to see a movie with me? I'll treat you to dinner and a movie and not at Jim's burger. I was thinking of going to Valiente's. Do you want to try that restaurant for a change? Wear your dress and fix up your hair and I'll dress up and we can go out and have a nice time. Wha - what do you think Ray? He stuttered.

Well it has been a while since I have been to the movies, she said. Sure, I'd love to go, it sounds like fun. She knew it sounded like a date but she convinced herself that it wasn't a date exactly, Because they were friends and friends don't date. They continued with their visit and toward the end Joe looked at her and asked, "How have you been?" I mean with the nightmares and the anger and all that. You know Joe, I haven't had hardly any nightmares in over a month and I am getting to the point where I don't really care about Richard and his stupid friends. They don't really seem to matter any more.

I get a little upset but I don't really care what happens to them. It is like they are just more jerks that are a part of my past. The hard part for me is that I can't seem to trust men in the present. Well, more than that I can't seem to trust my own judgment, She said sincerely. I worry about myself and that I can't really tell what kind of people surround me. I know you are my friend and Sandra is my friend but it is like I am always waiting for something to happen. I understand what you mean Ray. You have been hurt by people you have trusted, he said in a low tone. Yes Joe. My parents, my husbands and all of them. I haven't been hurt by everyone I have ever known but the few who have hurt me, really did hurt me a lot, she continued.

Well, I think you are a good person Ray, and you have had some bad judgment in the past with a few people but they helped to deceive you. You wanted to trust them and so you seen them as trustworthy. You won't make a mistake with everyone you meet now. I think you have begun to make a difference in your life. After all, you are friends with me and Sandra and there have been times when you would have trusted some pretty bad people but this year you didn't. You made good choices this year. I think things are a little more in perspective for you Ray. You just need to see it for yourself. When you realize these things for yourself you will understand, He said kindly.

They went on talking about church stuff and the meditation class. So are you about ready to help with the meditation class Ray? Reverend Charlene is about to Start her classes in just a month or two. She decided that the church can't wait for it much longer. Do you think you will be up to it? He asked. Sure, I am already settled into work and all. The only problem I can see is if she does the class during the day on my work days. She has been reserving the first room on the days of Mondays and Thursdays at 7pm until 8:30pm That will give enough time to do a full meditation and clear the room afterwards, he explained. Oh, that will be wonderfully perfect for me! She exclaimed.

It was getting late. It was almost 9pm when Joe said, we should be heading home soon Ray. I gotta get going; I have an early day tomorrow. Yep, me too Joe. I have to be at the store at 7am I better get home and get in bed. They got up and cleared the table then walked out together. He walked her to her car and they said good night. Raylynn offered him a hug and he held her tight for a few minutes. Raylynn loved the hug and she wanted to stay there in his arms all night but she knew she had to go home. She got into her car and started the engine and watched Reverend Joe walk to his car and get in. She slowly drove away.

She felt so strongly that he was a good man and that he could be trusted. She just wishes she could trust herself. She arrived at home before 9:30 and she went inside and changed into her pajamas and got ready for bed. She was actually happy and she was glad that she got to spend some time with Joe. She climbed into bed and drifted off to sleep in no time at all. She slept the whole night through although she had some strange dreams about werewolves attacking her church members. They all lived on the same property and the werewolves came in and started attacking everyone. After the dreams of the attacks she dreamed that they build defenses and was safe from the werewolves with minimal losses.

She woke up feeling refreshed and didn't even have much anxiety throughout the day. Wednesday went by smoothly and she enjoyed the Wednesday night service. Friday came with quickness and she was ready to go out after her counseling session. She met with Sara and they didn't have much to talk about. They discussed her feelings about her trusting herself and they talked about the day when she will be able to trust her choices. Sara explained that everyone is different and that some people never learn to trust their instincts while others learn very quickly. It all depends on how she sees life and how she sees other people. Being able to spot the red flags and loving herself enough to pay attention to them will all depend on her. Only she will be able to make that decision. It will be when she realizes her worth and her right to be treated with kindness and how well she learns to demand to be treated with kindness.

Some people never learn that while others learn quickly. The session ended well and they discussed that the time is coming near that they don't need to see each other as often anymore and they will eventually no longer need to see each other. She has been in counseling for almost 8 months and she has been working hard to get things straightened out. It took a long time to go over the time line and even longer to work out the issues but Raylynn was doing much better and should be able to face the rest of it alone.

They walked to the waiting room and said good bye. She was wearing her best dress and had her hair done up nicely and she even put on makeup before Joe came to pick her up so she was all ready to go out. She walked into the ladies room and reapplied her lipstick and her powder then walked out to meet Joe. Joe put his hand on her back and escorted her out of the clinic.

On their way to the car Raylynn mentioned that she was almost finished with her counseling visits and that they don't have another counseling visit for another 2 weeks then it will be a couple more sessions every 3 weeks after that. He looked at her with a grin and asked how she felt about that. You know, I was a little scared at first but then I realized I am okay with it. I don't feel the same way I did before and I actually feel stronger. I know eventually I will learn to trust myself and I don't think that Sara can help me with that. He grinned even bigger and said that's good Ray. I'm glad to hear that.

Do you think you will be ready to start seeing someone sooner or later? He asked. I don't know yet Joe. I need to learn how to trust my own judgment first, She replied.

Well, let's go get something delicious to eat and see a fun movie, he said. Sounds like a great night Joe, she said softly. She looked at him and thought he looked like he was up to something. They went to Valiente's Restaurant for dinner. They walked in and were seated almost immediately although the restaurant seemed a little busy. He had reservations and did a great job at impressing Raylynn that night. He was the perfect gentlemen and showed that he had enough class to be out in a more formal atmosphere. Raylynn hadn't been out to someplace nice like that since she was a young teenager. A four star restaurant like that was something she didn't think she would ever see again, especially with her wages. She was doing better for herself and she was even considering going to college to learn how to do bookkeeping and to be an administrative assistant. She always wanted to know how to do those sorts of things and wanted to know what it would be like to work in such a job as in an office.

She didn't know how long it would be before she could take the time to go through college and it was a bit scary to her just yet but she can dream about it. They had a wonderful Italian meal and even dessert. Raylynn loves Italian food but rarely eats pasta and tonight the meal was exquisite. They had great conversation as Joe always has been a great conversationalist. She believes that Joe has become a special part of her life and couldn't imagine him not being a part of it. They went to see a movie and it didn't even matter what movie it was, Raylynn was having the time of her life. It was like a date but it wasn't a date so it was safe.

The evening ended just as wonderfully as it began. Joe Took her home a little later than she wanted to stay out but still early enough to get some sleep before work tomorrow. He walked her to her door and Raylynn offered a hug and he held her tight. He inhaled her fragrance deeply and let her go. Goodnight Ray, he said then took his leave. She wanted to stand there in his arms a little longer but dared not say anything. She didn't want him to get the wrong idea and she wasn't ready for a relationship just yet. Saturday came and went. She didn't do anything for New Year's Eve this year any more than she did the year before or the year before that.

Sunday was New Year's day and she was planning to spend it with Reverend Joe in her little apartment. She would make lunch and dinner for them and they would watch the parade on television and take the decorations off the tree. Joe would be bringing the tree back to his place before church that night. He planned another heart felt movie for the little church. The members seemed to like the little movies he played and they always had a meaningful moral to end with. Saturday night Raylynn went to bed a little earlier than usual. She felt a little tired and just wanted to get some rest.

Saturday went by quickly and Raylynn went home to clean her apartment and get ready for Sunday. She planned to get up late eat breakfast and get ready for Joe to come over. She got home about 5:30 and made spaghetti for dinner then began cleaning by doing the dinner dishes. She swept the kitchen and dining room floor, vacuumed and dusted and straightened up. The only thing she couldn't do is the laundry because the laundry room was closed on New Year's Eve. The manager didn't want any of the kids using it as a party room like they did last year. She had her entire apartment clean as a whistle by 8:30 so she made herself some Chamomile tea and honey and sat down to relax. She watched a little television and admired the tree a little since it will be gone tomorrow.

Since Reverend Joe had planned to plant the tree in his backyard she was glad she could enjoy it over the holidays. She thought about tomorrow and wondered if she and Reverend Joe could ever be more than just friends. Would she be able to have a relationship and would he want to have one with her. It has been a long time since she has been in a relationship and the same seemed to be for him. It has been almost 6 years for her and almost as long for Reverend Joe. As far as she knows he hasn't dated anyone after his wife left and that was a few years ago. She couldn't help her feelings even if she was wrong about him being wonderful. She also couldn't help but feel like she couldn't have a deep and meaningful relationship after all that she has been through either. Maybe she is better off alone, At least being alone she won't get hurt again.

She shook off the thought and went about her night. She was going to try to stay up to watch the New York ball drop but before too long she was fast asleep on the sofa. She woke up about 12:30 with her empty tea cup in one hand and drool running down her chin. She didn't realize she drooled but found out that when she falls asleep sitting up she definitely drools. She got up feeling a little disappointed that she fell asleep and missed the ball drop. She missed the birth of the new year. She felt things were going to be different this year. This will be the first year after her raise and extra hours. She had room in her budget for extras. She was feeling stronger than she did before she started counseling with Sara. She wasn't quite sure what made the difference but she knew it absolutely made a difference in her life. She wasn't having nightmares like before and the anxiety was down. When she had a flashback she was able to manage it and it wasn't so shocking to her. Over all she was happier and having Sandra as a friend was a blessing. She kept her active with people and had her in the social mix. Then there was Joe. He has made a huge difference in her life this past year.

If it wasn't for Joe she would have never gone to counseling. She would have never done anything to change the way she was feeling and the way she seen life. She was most grateful for Joe. She didn't want to think of what life would be like without Joe in it. One thing's for sure; people seem to leave her life one way or another and it is likely that eventually Sandra and Joe will both be gone. Life will take them away somehow.

She got up and dragged herself into her room to try and go back to sleep. She climbed into bed and covered up. She laid there for a while thinking about her life and how things seem to be changing. She wondered what life had in store for her this year. She finally fell asleep. She had strange dreams of children playing and she was talking to a woman about her own age in part of the dream but when she awakened she couldn't remember what they were talking about.

She woke up about 9am and decided she better get moving. Joe was going to arrive about 1pm and she was expected to have lunch ready. She got up and took her shower, brushed her teeth and combed her hair then got dressed for the day. She went into the kitchen and made a pot of coffee and grabbed her fruit and cream. She sat at the kitchen table and ate her breakfast and drank a cup of coffee while she relaxed and got her brain in gear. She decided to see what was up online. She didn't spend a lot of time online but she often just sat and looked to see what everyone was up to. She didn't have any close friends other than Sandra and Joe and didn't really have any family to speak of since most of her family was jerks to begin with.

After a few minutes she realized there was nothing really interesting going on so she began her day by doing up the couple of breakfast dishes. She brought out the saved cartons for the tree decorations and had plenty of time to mull around. She decided to bring out her old journal that she used to write in a while back. She decided to make a new entry. She had grown tired of writing in it because she mostly whined about how terrible her life was. This entry would be different. She opened her journal to the next blank page and began. Dear Diary, Life has given me quite the trial and tribulation of experiences in my life but today I am going to have a great time with my newest friend Reverend Joe. Today we are going to undecorate the lovely tree that Joe brought over to share with me for the holidays. It is still his tree and he will be taking it home today but it is a real tree and I am grateful that I had such a magnificent tree in my home to enjoy.

I have been in counseling and although it started out horrific for me, I actually see improvement in my life. For the first time in my life I feel happy. I feel happy most of the time and that is an obvious change for me. She stopped and thought a minute. She used to be so sad. Life seemed to be against her all the time and now at least for now it seemed to be all for her. Sandra, Joe, Sara, and the promotion have all been good things in her life. She wrote, I am grateful for all of the little things and for the special people in my life. I am glad I have Sandra and Joe and I am glad Joe set me straight with counseling and got me interested. I don't think I would be as happy today if it wasn't for them.

Just then she heard a knock at the door. She looked at the clock and realized that a lot of time had passed but Reverend Joe wasn't supposed to be over for another hour. She got up and went to the door. Who is it? She called out. It's me Joe, she heard from the other side. She opened the door and there was Joe with a box. Come in, Raylynn said. Hi what's in the box? She asked with curiosity. Just then she heard some scratching noises and a meow. I was given a kitten by one of the church members but I can't keep it. I'm not home enough to care for a pet and I was wondering if you would be interested in taking care it for me. At first she felt a bit reluctant because she had no need to take care of another living creature until he opened the box and inside was a tiny little white kitten.

Raylynn's heart melted immediately. She reached in the box and picked it up. You look like a little snow ball, she said in a high pitch tone. You are so cuuute she said as if she were talking to a baby. If you want it, I have food and a cat pan and even litter in the car. I will go get them. I don't know Joe, a pet to care for; I haven't been good at taking care of living things. I will help with the expenses if that is a problem. Well, vet visits might be a problem. When the kitten gets old enough I will need some help getting it fixed and there is an issue with a pet deposit that is required here, she explained. No problem Ray, I can help with that, he said happily.

Okay, go get the stuff, she said. He ran back out to his car and grabbed all of the kitty supplies and brought them in. Raylynn took the cat pan and litter to the bathroom and set up the kitty's potty place. Okay kitty, the kitten had followed her into the bathroom and was watching what she was doing. She placed the kitten in the pan full of litter. Now this is where you go potty, okay Snowball. The kitten scratched around in the pan a little then hopped out and rubbed against Raylynn's ankle. Raylynn walked out to the kitchen again and went through the bag of stuff. There were the kitten's dishes, food and some toys. She spread the toys around the living room floor and set up the kitten's dishes with dry food and water. The kitten found the food and water quickly and took a drink. Raylynn asked Joe if he was hungry too but he didn't answer. He asked a question instead. So whatchya think of Snowball? Is Snowball a girl or a boy kitten? She replied. Well, the lady who gave him to me said Snowball was a girl, he replied. She is very cute. I hope she doesn't mind spending quite a bit of time alone, Raylynn whispered as if she didn't want Snowball to hear.

Reverend Joe looked at the kitten and up at Raylynn who was watching Snowball play with her toys. If you don't mind Ray I am a little hungry now. No problem I will get right to making lunch. She grabbed the bag of tomatoes out of the refrigerator and put on a pot of water to boil. What are you going to make for lunch Ray? He asked. Tomato soup and grilled cheese sandwiches from scratch, she replied. Oh that sounds wonderful he said as he stood by to watch how she was going to make it. They talked while Raylynn made lunch. She served it with cream and a grilled cheese on the side with a cup of coffee.

He sat down to eat lunch and looked at it with amazement. Wow Ray, when I was told you could cook I had no idea it was anything as awesome as this. He took a sip of his soup and a bite of grilled cheese. He sighed with contentment then he took another bite. This is amazing Raylynn, he said. Raylynn was a little flushed at the compliment and said "thank you Joe" as she grinned. After lunch they started on the tree. They took the decorations off one by one and placed them in the box. The kitten was having a blast playing with her toys and Raylynn's toes. They had a fun afternoon and they finished it off with a wonderful dinner of stuffed pork chops, baked potatoes and green beans.

They went to church that night and had a little party afterward. Raylynn had made an apple pie to bring for the dessert feast. Sandra was there as usual and made sure everyone knew that the delicious apple pie was made by Raylynn. Gerty asked Raylynn for her recipe which of course Raylynn gave her once before. Raylynn felt very happy as she left the church that night. Sandra was the only one who knew that Reverend Joe and Raylynn had spent the day together and she didn't tell anyone exactly. Sandra only hinted in the gossip that they might like each other and the plans to get the two together might be working. She went home that night and climbed into bed all snug and happy with Snowball laying next to her on her pillow.

Chapter 14

Meditation and Reverend Charlene

The year started out well and things seemed to be going pretty well. It's February and March is right around the corner. It begins to warm up around the middle of March in the western side of the states with all of the sunshine. The cold winter months are limited to about Three months out of the year for the cold and rainy season. The snow is limited to the foot hills and surrounding mountains leaving the valleys wet with rain. Raylynn seemed to be doing better every day and she seemed to get stronger as the days passed too. Reverend Charlene called Raylynn on Thursday, just a few days past Valentines Day.

Raylynn had made it a point not to celebrate Valentine's Day because of all of the hurt that had been caused in the past seemed to well up and ruin the day. If she made it through the day without recognizing it as a lover's day she would have a pretty good day. Joe was understanding and left her to be alone on Valentine's Day although it made him feel a bit sad to be alone on that day. He too had been hurt and Valentine's Day had a little bit of a sting to it so he left it alone. He was hoping to get Sandra and Raylynn together to do something fun that day but Raylynn had to work and just wanted to treat it like any other day.

When Reverend Charlene called Raylynn it was to begin making plans toward the Meditation class she was offering. She wanted Raylynn to memorize Short meditation stories to keep her on her toes. The first meditation was going to be a guided mediation and she wanted Raylynn to pay close attention to how it was done because she wanted her to do some of the guided meditations herself. Raylynn was a bit nervous about leading the meditations sometimes and filling in for Reverend Charlene from time to time. She realized that she was about to donate a great deal of her time toward the meditation class. The class would only be once a week but she would be available on Monday, Thursdays and Saturdays for anyone who needed help or needed to talk about meditation related issues.

The class was actually being assigned on Monday nights in the room next to the main hall. It was the Elements Room. It was decided that the 5 elements Earth, air, fire, water, and spirit were perfect to help keep balance in meditation and the room was beautifully decorated to keep the reminders of the elements fresh in the mind. When first entering the room to the left is the element of earth, lovely vines and other indoor plants occupy this wall. Straightforward is the element of air with birds and butterflies painted on the wall in a beautiful mural depicting the creatures of the air. To the right is fire with the sun hanging on the wall on one side and the moon on the other side of the wall. The wall with the door is the element of water. A beautiful statuette of dolphins set next to the door on one side with Wales on the other. The center of the room is spirit and on the floor was a white rug laying over plush carpet. The purpose of the elements was to help the mind focus and get centered. Each wall would be a great focal point for meditation Reverend Charlene explained. Raylynn began to become excited with the up and coming classes. The new Meditation classes were going to start the First week of March which was just about two weeks away.

When Reverend Charlene was finished discussing the plans for the class they said their goodbyes and hung up. Raylynn jumped up and waltzed around the room once then gave a bit of a giggle. This is going to be fun Snowball. She said as she picked up the growing kitten. She sat on the sofa and petted Snowball for a few. Snowball loved the attention. She really seemed to enjoy Raylynn's affections and Raylynn was happy to spend time with her. Snowball sat on her lap for quite some time before she decided to get up and move down onto the sofa. Raylynn has grown quite fond of the kitten and couldn't imagine how she could live life without her. She enjoyed her time spent with the kitten watching her play with her toys. She has even purchased a few new toys including a scratching post and some catnip to draw her away from clawing the furniture.

Before long it was bedtime so Raylynn got ready and climbed in bed. She slept well but had a few strange dreams about getting lost on a train. It wasn't a scary type of dream just a curious type. She ended up in Canada on the train and she transferred once following a man she had given directions to but had lost him.

Apparently he was better at following directions than she was. It was pouring rain when she got off the train and there were wolves and tigers tied to fences in people's yards with a dead cat and a dead dog laying on the side of the road. When she asked what happened to them the driver who picked her up and offered her a ride said they were tragic losses. The driver who was then a woman had a beauty salon in her vehicle but Raylynn had a feeling not to step inside so she made an excuse as to why she couldn't at the time. Then her dream switched to her parents and they were angry with her because she didn't make dinner yet.

She woke up from this dream about the time she was about to eat a chocolate covered graham cracker. What a strange set of dreams she thought. They seem to have no bearing on reality like her nightmares did. They didn't make sense at all. She couldn't follow her dreams any more and she didn't quite know what to think of them. She wasn't quite sure what the getting lost and ending up in Canada had to do with anything. Maybe it was just her creative side of her brain making up stuff for a change and it didn't have anything to do with reality. She thought about the dream books and thought that just for fun she would look them up. But what would she look up? Tigers, wolves, getting lost, and trains she wasn't quite sure. She looked each of them up and they didn't make any sense to her, not as combined anyway. She knew she was on a new journey through life and that it was a path that she had never taken before. Maybe that was the trip and the animals were different aspects of inner self. Maybe she needed to let go a little and untie the wild side and let the tame side go for a change; take some chances.

She giggled at the thought of her wild side. She didn't even know what her wild side was. She was always holding back because she didn't know what kind of trouble she might find next. She picked herself up off the floor and put her laptop on the table. She got up and got ready for work. She thought about the dream all day and her conclusion of course. Since she has never been on this road of life before the one of healing she was kind of lost because it wasn't familiar to her. She knew healing was her destination but since she had never been there before she didn't know what to expect. She was to see Sara Today. It was going to be the last time she is to see her. Maybe she should discuss her idea about the dream with her and see what she has to say about it.

She went to work as usual and got off at 1pm as usual. Now that I'm not going to be seeing Sara anymore I wonder what I will do with my time. Maybe the meditation class issues will fill the day, She thought. Maybe she will just relax or maybe she can spend it with Joe. Joe had Friday afternoon off maybe just maybe he will want to spend the afternoon with her. She went home after work feeling kind of abandoned by Sara. She didn't quite know why, she always knew it would only be for a little while and it has been almost a year since she started seeing her. She was afraid, what if the nightmares come back? What if I am only taking a break from the anxiety and it all comes crashing back? What will I do then? She was worried about all of the “what ifs” but she bravely made her pot of coffee, washed her face and hands and changed her clothes.

She sat at the dining table and just relaxed while drinking her coffee while waiting for Joe. Since she was getting more restful sleep she didn’t feel as tired these days but it was nice to just sit and relax. Before long it was about 3:30 and Joe was knocking at the door. She got up and walked slowly to the door. She opened it and greeted Joe with an expression of sadness. What’s the matter Ray? He asked with concern. What’s bothering you. I won’t be seeing Sara anymore and I can’t help but feel a little sad. What if all the bad things come back on me. What if I start having nightmares again and the anxiety gets bad again. What do I do? She said sadly.

You will be fine Ray, really. You don’t have anything to worry about, he said. You have me and Sandra if you really need to talk about something. We don’t mind listening you know. We are your friends and we care about you, he explained. Well I don’t know why I feel so sad and I feel like I am being abandoned. Like I am just being sent out to the wolves to fend for myself. What if I am not ready? She whined. You are ready to be on your own, she wouldn’t let you go if you weren’t ready, he said reassuringly. I guess you’re right but I can’t help how I feel. Well talk to her about it Ray. Just let her know how you feel and listen to what she has to say.

They walked out of the apartment and got in his car and drove to the clinic. As they pulled up to the clinic

Raylynn's heart began to sink. She dreaded these visits in the beginning. It was difficult to tell her story then but she has since grown to feel good about the visits as she seen things happening in her life that she thought would never be possible. Today was going to be the last day that she will see Sara whom she had began to depend on for support and someone whom she could confide in to talk about all the stuff that bothers her. Sara knew all of her secrets. It was all the things that no one person knew that she told Sara. Her deepest darkest secrets about the rapes and the molestation and the abuse she endured at the hands of her mother that she confided in Sara.

Now her life has changed and it's time for Sara to leave her life. What an impact this woman has had on her to help her through such difficult times. Now she was going to be gone and Raylynn didn't know if she was going to go on being okay or she would need her again. Raylynn thought for a moment as they got out of the car and said out loud I guess if I need a counselor again I can always find one somewhere. Joe listened to her but he knew she wasn't really talking to him or to anyone really. He just walked her in silence into the clinic. She went inside and walked up to the desk and checked in as usual while Reverend Joe found them a seat near the door where Sara would call her name.

They waited in silence as the time ticked by until Sara opened the door and called her name. She walked to Sara and they continued down the hall to her office. They stepped inside and Raylynn took a look around one last time. She wanted to remember this room. She wanted to remember everything that happened in this room. All the times that she cried and every time she choked out one of the stories. She felt like she was leaving a piece of herself behind in these four walls behind this closed door.

Then she realized she was leaving a piece of herself behind. She was leaving the pain and the torment behind. She was leaving the self doubt and negative self talk behind. Most of all she was leaving with new hope, new found inspiration and above all else she was bringing with her a new sense of self worth which was more than she ever hoped for. She knew she was worthy of being happy and being loved. Sara asked how she was doing and she said, you know Sara, I was sad today that I wouldn't be seeing you any more and I was afraid for what the future will bring without you to talk to but I realized it's okay to leave the past behind me with you in this office. I know I am going to be okay now and if I need help in the future I will have that somewhere out there.

Sara looked at her and smiled and said yes Raylynn, you will be just fine. You have come a long way and you will go even farther on your own. I am letting you go because I know you are ready. I think you arc rcady to face the world on your own with a new chance to live well. You are right about counseling. There are counselors out thcrc and they will help you whcn you need it and Raylynn, keep in mind that Joe is a true friend to you. He has some training in my field and will always do in a pinch. Sara went over the last several months and they talked about where she can go from where she was in life. Sara told her that she has some things to deal with but she was ready to deal with them on her own. She told her she has grown stronger and that she is ready for anything that comes her way. She gave her some reassurance that she was going to be fine on her own now.

After the session she felt better about it and was happier than when she went in. They said their goodbyes and Raylynn thanked Sara for everything she has helped her with. She didn't quite know how the changes happened only that they did and for that she was grateful. Raylynn walked over to Joe and said "let's get out of here" with a great big smile and Joe knew she was going to be fine. Well Joe what are we going to do after this? You won't need to come pick me up anymore. Are you going to be gone too? She asked. You can't get rid of me that easily Ray, he said with a chuckle. I was thinking, since you are done with counseling and you seem to be doing better with stuff in your life, how do you feel about dating? I don't really know Joe, let me think about it for a while and I will let you know how I feel about it. Who do you have in mind for me to date? She asked curiously.

Well, um, Ray, he stammered, I was thinking about me he said as he blushed. Raylynn smiled and threw her arms around him and gave him a great big hug. You are wonderful Joe, she said as she hugged him. If you are asking me to go steady I am going to have to really think about it and I will get back with you about how I feel about it. Okay? She said with a serious expression. Okay Ray, you go ahead and think about it. I won't bring it up again until you bring it up first, he said heavily. I won't keep you waiting any longer than I have to Joe, I promise, she said softly. Okay, how about some dinner Ray. I will take you out anywhere you wanna go, he said with a smile. How about Jim's Burgers to celebrate my new life with a big shebang and I'll pay this time. I'd like to have ice cream for dessert my treat, she said excitedly.

So that is just what they did. They went to Jim's burgers and Raylynn asked Joe to go find a seat that tonight was on her. She ordered their bacon cheeseburgers with Hot coffee. She stopped and picked up creamer and sugar on her way to the table. He picked a table near the window and they had a good time. She wanted to go to Cooglie Goops ice cream parlor for ice cream. She went to a party there when she was a little girl and it was one of the best times she ever had. They had Ice cream and cake and the little birthday girl was very nice to her. That was a big deal because kids were not usually very nice to Raylynn back then. She ordered an ice cream sundae and he ordered a banana split. The servings were huge and they had a great time joking and talking about happy memories.

Raylynn didn't have a lot of good memories but now she can remember the good times because the bad times aren't such an overshadow hiding the good times. She went home happy as happy can be. He walked her to her door and said good night. He wanted to kiss her but he knew he shouldn't push things as it is. He wanted to give her some space to come to terms with what she wanted on her own. She gave him a big hug and said thanks for spending the time with her. He went home and she went inside. She walked over to the sofa where Snowball was laying and sat down. She picked up the kitten and placed her on her lap and began to pet her. Well snowball, what do you think of Joe? Sara said I should trust him and he asked me to be his girlfriend tonight. I don't know what I should do. Snowball just purred and licked her paw.

She had to really think about it. She really liked Joe and if she were to have a relationship he would be perfect for one. They always had a good time together and she didn't ever want him to leave her life. What should she do? She went to bed thinking about it. She lay in bed and wondered what it would be like to be in a relationship with Joe. She was guessing it would be different because he is so different from any of the other guys she has ever been with. He is nice and kind. He is the most giving guy she has ever met but she still wasn't sure if she was ready for a relationship. The arguments and having to spend time together were always a problem in her past relationships. They spent time together anyway and they have yet to have a fight. She drifted off to sleep in no time. She woke up to her alarm clock right on time.

The next two weeks went by really quickly and Raylynn was having trouble making up her mind. It was Monday, time for her first Meditation class. She got ready and went to the church. Reverend Charlene did a beautiful guided meditation after she gave a brief instruction on how to begin meditation. They did the cleansing breaths and went through the meditation without a problem. She spoke clearly and smoothly while Raylynn watched her walk around the room speaking softly and calmly. She did it all from memory. Raylynn watched around the room. Some of the class was clearly having trouble getting comfortable.

After the class she spoke with Reverend Charlene about the meditation she did. She wanted to know where she could find beautiful guided meditations like that. Reverend Charlene told her she wrote most the ones she used. She told her she wanted to take turns doing them for the class and handed her a couple of books to get an idea of what to do. Raylynn was worried but she was excited about next week. Reverend Charlene said it would be easier to remember the meditation if she wrote it. She went home and browsed through the books to get an idea of what she was looking at. She grew tired quickly and decided to just get ready for bed and look at the books tomorrow. She hopped in bed with her new volunteer work on her mind. Her phone number has been given out to people with her hours of availability. Would she get many calls and if so what would they be like? She thought about the new class and her responsibility until she drifted off to sleep.

Tuesday went by as normal and Tuesday evening she met with Joe like clockwork. She told Joe all about the exciting parts of the new meditation classes. Joc just sat there and smiled as shc told about it. When she was finished telling about the first day of class and how wonderful Reverend Charlene was Joe just nodded and said “I’m glad you are enjoying your new adventure with the class. Teaching others how to meditate can be a blessing in their lives. Everyone who has an interest in meditation can benefit greatly from the relaxation techniques of meditation". Raylynn nodded in agreement and said, "I know for a fact meditation helps because it helps me every day". Now all she needs to do is take a few cleansing breaths and she feels good as new.

They talked for a while. Raylynn truly enjoyed that Joe sat and talked to her. She didn't know any other guys who would ever sit and just have a conversation with her. She was impressed with how well she got along with him and how well he could hold up his end of the conversations. She liked the fact that he seemed to listen most all; at least for the most part. They didn't have many conversations over the phone but they did share quite a bit of time together in person having hours of wonderful talks about almost anything. Joe was happy that she was enjoying the new class as he knew she would. He suggested her in the clergy meeting about the class. Reverend Charlene wanted one of the clergy to help but he suggested Raylynn because she needed the responsibility as well as the opportunity to discover the potential within her.

She found time to look at the books and she wrote a meditation of her own. She didn't do as great of a job at it on her first time guiding the meditation. She was very nervous and couldn't remember some of it. Her voice was shaky and she hesitated for a while. Reverend Charlene told her she did a good job for her first time and reassured her that after doing it a few times she wouldn't be as nervous about it. She would become more comfortable and her confidence would grow. Raylynn trusted Reverend Charlene and told her she knew what she was saying was true but she was glad this time was over with. Reverend Charlene encouraged her not to quit and of course Raylynn said she is nowhere near giving up.

Raylynn went home and thought about what she had done in the class and how she could improve her methods. She decided that for the next few turns she would have her guided meditation written and typed as an easy to read guideline until she could relax and remember it on her own and her self confidence was boosted enough to help her complete them without the need for the written version. She asked Reverend Charlene if that would be okay and she agreed that it might be a good idea at first and most everyone should have their eyes closed so they won't really know that she is reading. Raylynn agreed and they didn't have any more problems with Raylynn's guided meditations. Of course at first Reverend Charlene decided to take two turns to Raylynn's one turn.

The class grew and they all got to know one another over the course of the class. They planned the class to last until the end of summer then they would begin a new beginner meditation class. The new meditation class they would have guests from the first class come and perform the guided meditation for the class to give them a break. Joe kept his word and didn't say anything about his proposal for Raylynn to be his girlfriend. He just kept being the same great guy he always was. Raylynn couldn't let herself go and have a relationship just yet. She was still afraid that she couldn't handle it.

One day she was sitting there in the coffee shop waiting for Joe to come with the coffee and the sandwiches and she was watching him. She thought about the past year of them meeting on a regular basis and she thought about the counseling sessions. Was she doomed to be alone the rest of her life? She realized at that moment that she would only be alone if she chose to be. She realized that she was capable of having a relationship and that essentially she and Reverend Joe were already seeing each other but it hasn't been made official.

She realized at that moment as she watched him carry the tray with coffee and sandwiches over to the counter to grab the cream and sugar that she was already in love with this man. She realized that she was ready to help others and this meditation class proved it to her. She watched him as he walked over to the table and as he put the tray down. She looked up at him smiling. He looked at her and said "What?" "Why are you smiling at me like that". She said do you remember when you asked me to be your girlfriend? Yep, he replied although he seemed to be a little stunned that she remembered. Are you still interested in being my boyfriend? She asked. Well, yes Ray I would really like for us to be officially dating. I really don't want to go on for the rest of my life being just your friend.

Well, I have been thinking about it and I am thinking that I am ready for a relationship if you still want to have one with me. He gave her a big smile and kissed her on the hand. Ray we have been seeing each other for over a year now. I have been waiting patiently for you since the day I met you. I love you Ray and I'm glad that you are ready to be my girlfriend. I hope that someday you will love me as much as I love you. You hold my heart and I would love to hold yours. They spent the rest of the date planning what they should do on Friday and how they should plan to date. They decided nothing would change and they would continue to see each other and have a special date every Friday. Friday would be date night.

When they parted that night they walked out of the Dark Roast hand in hand. He walked her to her car and gave her a big hug and a kiss on the cheek. She didn't know what to think of that considering she just told him she would be his girlfriend and he kissed her on the cheek. He helped her into her car and said good night. Reverend Joe walked to his car smiling all the while. He was happy she wanted to be his girlfriend but he was waiting for her to fall in love with him before he gave her a real kiss. He wanted her to be sure about her choice before he made the move.

Friday arrived and Raylynn got up with time to spare. She got ready for work and decided she was going to wear something a little more appealing on their date. Maybe jeans and T-shirt aren't exactly kissing cloths, she thought. She looked through her closet which the contents have grown over the last several months. She decided that she didn't have anything suitable and she would have to go shopping after work.

Since Friday was date night Joe wouldn't be by to pick her up until 6pm and she had plenty of time to stop off and buy something nice and a little more appealing. When she got off at 1pm she went to several shops before she found the outfit that she wanted to wear on her date. The top was lacey and feminine and instead of buying slacks she purchased a skirt that was just above her knee. She wanted to show off her sexy knee without seeming too forward in appearance. She wasn't offering the whole prize just wanting to be kissed.

She loved this man and he said he loved her so what was the problem. Didn't he know how she felt about him? She thought about it and realized she really didn't show much emotion when they had their conversation. She didn't tell him that she loved him although he professed his love for her. She knew she loved him. She has loved him for some time she just didn't know until recently. She got home about 4:00 that Friday afternoon and hurried to get ready. She took another shower to be fresh and clean and pulled her hair up with little wisps of hair flowing down around her face. She put on makeup and her clothes. She even put on pantyhose and her sandals with the high heel. She took a look at herself in the long mirror in her room and decided she looked her best. She loved her new clothes and thought she looked nice.

6pm and Joe arrived right on time. He was always right on time. She couldn't remember a time when he was late without calling her. She opened the door and invited Joe inside. He looked her over and whistled. Wow, Ray, you look beautiful tonight, he exclaimed.

She blushed for a minute then replied. I wanted to look nice for my boyfriend tonight on our first official date. He said he didn't expect it and that she was amazing. She looked at him in the eye with a serious expression and said "Joe, I didn't tell you before and I am not sure why but I wanted to tell you that......I Love you". He looked at her for a second as the words sank in and tears formed in his eyes. He reached out and pulled her close, his heart filled with joy, he leaned forward and pressed his lips against hers. Raylynn knew at that moment she would be fine from now on and that she could trust Joe with her heart no matter what.

***

About the Author

T. Kay Houston grew up in Southern California with her parents and 4 siblings. From a small child and until her 40th birthday she has experienced events that has impacted her life and inspired her to write Raylynn's Dark Secret. At age 30 she was diagnosed with Hypothyroidism which was later diagnosed as Hashimoto's Disease. She has since found that writing is her outlet to tell her stories. She believes that her stories have purpose in this world and hopes that Raylynn's Dark Secret will encourage more victims to come forward and tell their stories to counselors who may help them in the healing process. T. Kay Houston has three sons and four grandchildren all of whom hold her heart. She has her own Reverend Joe who helped her seek healing and guided her on her own path toward a new life.

Connect with the author
www.tkayhouston.com

Made in the USA
Columbia, SC
22 May 2024

36054602R00155